P9-CFP-704

Anna Jean Bennett Ditty

BACK IN WEST VIRGINIA SERIES

BOOK 2

Movin'

by Anna Jean Bennett Ditty

©2006 Anna Jean Bennett Ditty

ISBN 0-9759262-1-7

Table of Contents

Anna Jean (left) and Charlotte, 1935

Dedication

To my sister, Charlotte

I am dedicating this book to Charlotte. She was by my side, both literally and figuratively, every step of the way. It is as much hers as it is mine. We spent the summer months together for the past few years because we realized that time was running out for us, and we wanted to be together as much as possible. Oh, I'm so glad we did. These past several years have renewed and strengthened the strong bond that has always been there. I got unlimited long-distance service, so we could talk every day as long as we wanted. And we did.

My sister Charlotte died unexpectedly May 1, 2005, and left a void in my life. We had always been closer than sisters; we were friends, best friends. Ever since we were wee little, we had this closeness. She was injured so badly when she was 5 and I was 3. She spent two years in and out of hospitals, and I always felt I had to take care of her. We slept together till we grew up and left home. I would wrap myself around her back every night, like spoons nesting together (spoon buddies). I'd put my arm over her, and we would talk and talk and talk. All through our lives we have had this mutual admiration for each other. She has been my greatest fan, and I always thought she was so pretty and smart.

We were very different from one another in a lot of ways. She was little, pretty, smart, cocky and had gobs of beautiful, copper-red hair. She loved to read and had her nose in a book every chance she got. She loved music, especially opera. She had a lovely clear soprano voice and was crazy about Pavarotti. She sang in the church choir for more than 50 years. She could dance like you wouldn't believe. I remember her Jitter Buggin' at school dances and during the war years at the USO. Guys would stand in line to dance with her because she made them look good.

She graduated a year ahead of me (1943) and worked for Armour Meat Packing Co. as a bookkeeper for a year until I graduated in 1944. We left Hinton together and went to Hampton, Va. Charlotte took a Civil Service test and worked for the government for a year. Then we both went to work for the Bell Telephone Co. Charlotte met and married a soldier from Boston, Mass. They had two children, Karen and Rick. The marriage didn't work out, so they divorced soon after Rick was born.

She was a good mother and worked hard to provide for her children. She also adopted two of our cousin's little girls, who would have been placed in an orphanage. She worked for a couple of real estate agencies until Mommy had a stroke. She quit public work and became an independent Realtor and cared for Mommy for nine years. She bought several houses and put all four of her children through college. They moved to Buckroe in one of the houses that she owned about three blocks from the beach. We spent as much time as possible visiting back and forth when our children were growing up. My children loved her and looked forward to going to Buckroe every summer.

Charlotte was a good Christian and never missed church. She brought her children up in the fear and admonition of the Lord as scripture demands. She practiced what she preached. I am sure that she is in Heaven with our mother and that I will be reunited with them one day.

Anna Jean (left) and Charlotte, 2004

*Photos of Charlotte
through the years.*

Decades of Life

By Anna Jean Bennett Ditty

When you are ten and yet a child
Life is long and free and wild.
You play and sing and laugh and run
And everything you do is fun.

When you are twenty and still so young;
Your spirit's free and so is your tongue.
You live and love and laugh and think
That the fountain of youth is yours to drink.

When you are thirty and still have youth,
You begin to wonder and search for truth.
You work and laugh along the way
You're storing wisdom for a rainy day.

When you are forty and in your prime,
You know by now your foe is time.
You still can laugh and you still have life
But gone is youth's oblivion to strife.

When you hit fifty and most folks do;
Now it's a horse of another hue.
Though life seems sweet, it's not a lark
The odds bar you from the century mark.

Then comes sixty, the September time,
Your golden days so goes the rhyme.
There's more behind you than ahead
And more to life than your daily bread.

If you are lucky and seventy you see
You face the facts as the facts may be.
For now there is no time to plan;
Your future now is in your hand.

Some eighties and nineties there always are
Who wait around to cross the bar
These aged folks by now must know
From whence they came, they soon must go.

From youth to age the cycle flows;
From birth to death and so life goes.
An endless pattern is not God's plan;
The future starts with the death of man.

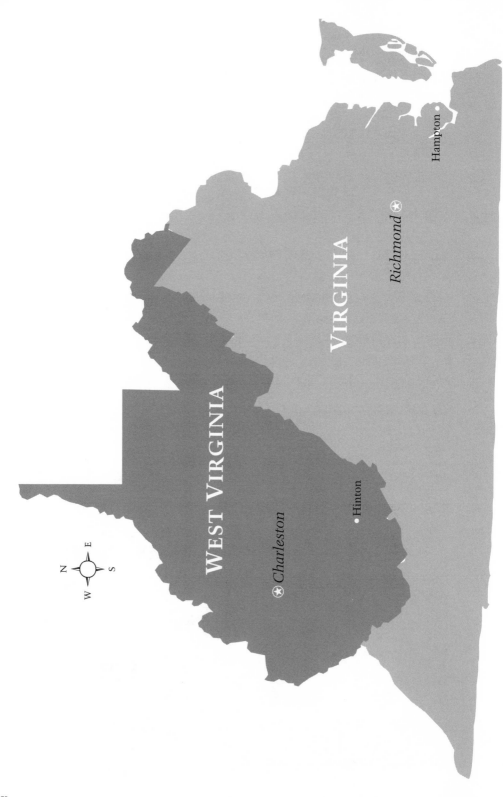

Family Tree

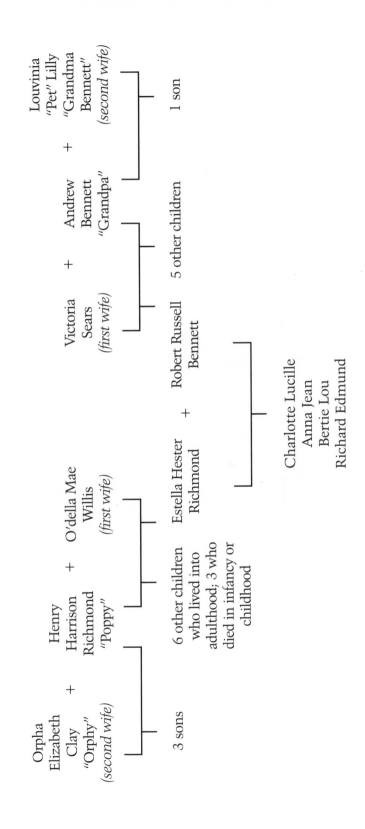

Orpha Elizabeth Clay "Orphy" *(second wife)* + Henry Harrison Richmond "Poppy" + O'della Mae Willis *(first wife)*

3 sons

6 other children who lived into adulthood; 3 who died in infancy or childhood

Estella Hester Richmond + Robert Russell Bennett

Victoria Sears *(first wife)* + Andrew Bennett "Grandpa" + Louvinia "Pet" Lilly "Grandma Bennett" *(second wife)*

5 other children

1 son

Charlotte Lucille
Anna Jean
Bertie Lou
Richard Edmund

CHAPTER *1*

The Move

I don't know why I felt so sad while my cousins, Joe and Alvin, were unloading the truck and bringing all our furniture and belongings down to the big, green, two-story house on 11th Avenue. I was huddled in the corner of the front porch steps. I had my knees up under my chin and my red and white, polka-dot dress pulled down over my legs as they went by carrying things in.

Some of the furniture they took into the house, and some of it they just set on the porch or in the yard. The truck was parked up in the alley where Grandma Bennett lived. They had to carry everything down a path to the cement walk in front of the house just above ours, then down four steps to the cement walk at our house.

Moving is sometimes a hard thing to do. Just the word "move," or some form of it, denotes different things but always some sort of a change: from one place to another, from one thing to another, from one situation to another. It's a verb: move the chair to the other side of the room, move out of town, move out of the country, move over, move on, move to tears. It's a noun: a boy can put the move on a girl, make your move in a game as in checkers, that was some move as in a ball game, smart move in business, etc. Get the picture?

I was bewildered by my feelings of sadness when we moved down to 11th Avenue from the house on the hill. I should have been delighted. It was, after all, a much better and bigger house and was definitely in a better, if not the best, part of town. No longer were we living on the outskirts of nowhere. No, we were finally down in the town where we could be proud to say we lived on 11th Avenue. But I was leaving the only real home I had ever known.

It was Saturday morning, and the sun was shining brightly. It was such a nice, warm, peaceful day that it was hard to imagine that our lives had been turned upside down and inside out in such a short period of time. It had rained steadily for several days in a row, and the house on the hill on Ninth Avenue that we had called home was no more. It literally had slid down off the hill to the road below and was now in the process of being demolished.

We had been staying with our Grandpa and Grandma Bennett, who lived on 10th Avenue, while arrangements could be made to move us to a new location. This big house was a darned sight nicer than the one on the hill, but that

The house on 11th Avenue as it looks today.

had actually been the only place we had ever called home. We had shifted about from one place to another since long before my memory kicked in.

Mommy and Daddy had lived with Grandpa and Grandma Bennett for the first few years of their marriage. Daddy had trouble keeping a job because of his drinking. His Aunt Laurie Pruce got Daddy to move us to Detroit, Mich., for awhile, and we lived with her. Daddy had a job there as a butcher, but when the Depression hit the country in 1929, he got laid off. He couldn't find another job, so we moved back to Hinton. We moved back in with Grandma and Grandpa Bennett. Daddy was drinking heavily, Mommy got pregnant again and Charlotte was struck by a car and was severely injured and was in the hospital. Daddy signed papers and got $600 from the woman who had hit Charlotte. He took most of it and went on the biggest drunken binge of his life. This was the last straw in a marriage that had been shaky for some time. Mommy packed up and moved in with Aunt Dilly and Uncle Arlie over in Smith Hollow. So when we moved to the house on the hill, we had, for the first time, a home of our own at last. Now another move. This house was a stark contrast to the one on the hill. For one thing, it had a front door and a back door both with porches. It was setting between two other houses, the same as the house we had left. In front of each house there was a cement walk with several steps; then a platform, more steps and another platform, then a long row of steps down to the street. The houses were built between the alley where Grandma lived and Temple Street.

Mommy had gone to work at the sewing factory early in the morning. Aunt Dilly was racing around like a chicken with its head cut off and squawking like a stuck pig. She had to be the most ungodly loud woman that God put on this earth. She was always yelling about something, and usually it wasn't anything of major proportions. Frankly, she yelled so much about everything that no one paid much attention to anything she said. She was a very good woman though, and very emotional, but she just went off on her tangents too often to be effective. She had been a part of our lives ever since I could remember, and we all loved her. We had lived with her over in the hollow when my little brother was born, and she had moved with us to the house on the hill. She had three rooms downstairs, and we had four rooms upstairs. She helped look after us while Mommy worked.

She and Mommy had been up all night helping Uncle Arlie, Poppy and my cousins, Joe and Alvin, get our things out of the house on the hill and into the truck that brought them down to our new house. Actually, it wasn't really a new house, but it was new to us. Mommy had made Charlotte and me help with a lot of the bags of clothes and bed covers and other things we could carry. We had been lugging bags of stuff from the old house down to the new one all day the day before. We went to Grandma Bennett's house for supper and slept there like we had done since the mud slide.

Aunt Dilly came flying out of the house and yelled at me, "Anna Jean, get up off your butt, and quit your mopin'. We all got lots of work to do. Now get in that kitchen, and start unpacking some of them dishes, and wash 'em and put 'em in the cupboard."

I knew better than to argue with Aunt Dilly, so I slowly pulled myself off the steps and opened the front door. There was a stairway with a mahogany railing to the left of the hall and a window at the foot of the stairs. On the right was a door to a room that was to become Mommy's bedroom. At the end of the hall was the door that opened into one big room that was the entire width of the house with windows at each end. This was to be our living room. From this room I went into what would be our dining room and into the kitchen on the left.

There were cardboard boxes stacked all over the floor, so I went over and opened the top one. Sure enough, there were dishes in there. I quietly slipped out the backdoor and ran up the hill to Grandma Bennett's. I didn't want to wash any old dishes, especially not by myself. I wanted to find Charlotte, my older sister. I had a feeling she was hiding somewhere with her nose in a book. She was the readingest

Grandma Bennett

person I'd ever seen. She would read anything and everything. I guess that was why she was so smart in school.

Grandma was outside cleaning a chicken. She had a dishpan sitting on an old wooden chair without a back on it. She had picked the feathers off the chicken, singed it and was washing it with homemade soap and a brush.

Its feet and head were still on, and it looked so funny lying there naked with its head lolling to one side and its feet sticking out stiff as a board. Now I know where the expression "naked as a picked bird's tail" came from. She looked up when I got near the porch.

"How come you ain't down there helpin' Dilly like you're supposed to?" she asked me.

"I'm lookin' for Charlotte." I mumbled defensively. "Aunt Dilly wants me to wash dishes, and Charlotte is supposed to help me. Do you know where she is?"

"Last time I seen her, she was on the front porch with Bertie and Dickie."

I watched Grandma scrub the chicken for a couple of minutes. Then she put it in a bucket of clean water she had setting by the chair. She picked up the dishpan and walked up the yard apiece and gave the pan a heave and sent the water flying through the air. She came back over and rinsed off the chicken.

Grandma had her hair pulled back in a big bun and was wearing one of Grandpa's old blue shirts over her nightgown. She was a short, fat, little woman, but she was always in a good mood. Nothing seemed to bother her. She lifted the chicken out of the water and lay it on the chair. She took a big butcher knife and whacked off its feet and head. Then she sliced it open at the butt end and pulled out all its guts and put them in the dishpan beside the chair. She put it back in the bucket of water and swished it around a couple of times. Neither one of us said anything. She worked on that chicken, and I watched, fascinated. After she had it rinsed off, she pulled it out of the bucket and held it up with both hands, so the water could drip off of it. She reached out and handed that big, old, wet chicken to me.

"Take it in the kitchen, and put it in the sink," she said without looking at me. She picked up the bucket of water and the pan of guts and headed up over the hill. I held the big rooster with one hand and opened the screen door with the other and went into the kitchen and flopped him in the sink that was right behind the door. Then I went through the house to the front porch. I still had to find Charlotte, and there she was, sitting in Grandpa's big, old, rocking chair, engrossed in a book, as usual.

"Aunt Dilly says we have to wash all them dishes and put 'em in the cupboard. She told me to find you and make you help me," I lied. Aunt Dilly had told me no such thing, but I was sure she would have if she'd thought of it.

Charlotte stuck her finger on the line where she was reading, so she wouldn't lose her place, and looked up. Charlotte was almost two years older than I was, but she was smaller. She had beautiful red hair, and it was getting longer than she usually wore it. She had been in and out of hospitals since she was 5 years old and was just now catching up. She was 10, and I was 8. We were very close, as we had slept together since we were wee little. She folded down the corner of the book and got up. We went down the hill and snuck in the back door, so Aunt Dilly wouldn't see us. She already thought I was busy washing dishes. It was just a matter of time till she would check on us, and we had better get to work.

I ran a pan of hot water and squished a bar of Octagon soap around in it until I got some suds. Then I opened one of the boxes of dishes, put them in the pan and started washing them. Charlotte filled another pan with hot water. As I washed the dishes and put them in the rinse water, Charlotte took them out and dried them. We were both amazed at the fact that we could turn on the spigot and get hot water. This was new to us. We always had a coal stove everywhere we lived, and we had to heat water for everything. Down here we had a gas stove, a gas water heater and gas heaters in all the rooms to keep us warm. We could take a bath with hot water in a real bathtub instead of the old zinc wash tub.

We washed and dried all the dishes that were in those old boxes and put them up in the cupboard. We hauled the boxes out on the back porch, and again we marveled that we had a back porch to put stuff on. There was a narrow cement walk going from the back porch to the front of the house, and there was a small, grassy yard on either side of the walk. This was also something new to us. We'd never had much of a yard before. There were wooden steps going up the side of the house to the upstairs and yet another porch. Wow!

We went back in the kitchen and swept the floor and mopped up the mess we had made doing the dishes. We really didn't want to do anything else, but we knew if Aunt Dilly caught us, we'd be busy all day. We decided to just take off, but as soon as we went out the back door, she caught us. She must have been watching us all along.

"Don't you two get no ideas about sneakin' off," she yelled. Them beds have been set up in the rooms upstairs, and you can just get up there and put the sheets on 'em and get 'em ready to sleep in tonight. Hester's gonna have enough to do when she gets home without you all making work for her. We gotta get this place in some kind of order."

We weren't too happy about the whole business, but up we went. Not very fast, but we went with her still yelling after us.

"Don't be draggin' your feet. Get them beds made, and get back down here. There's plenty of work to be done." Yak, yak, yak.

We went up the side stairs and into the room that was to become Joe and Alvin's bedroom. There were just a lot of boxes of stuff piled in it for the time being. We went through another room and into what was going to be Charlotte's, Bertie's, Marie's and my bedroom. There were two double beds in this room. We dug the sheets, blankets and spreads out of some boxes and made both beds.

We didn't want to, but we figured we'd better make the bed up in the other room too, or we'd be getting heck from

Aunt Dilly. This was where Uncle Arlie and Aunt Dilly were going to sleep. We were sorta' getting into the fixing up and decided to dig our clothes out of the boxes and hang them up in a closet. Yea, a closet — something we had never had before. We were pretty proud of ourselves and stood back and admired our new room. It was looking good. All we needed to do was get rid of some of the empty boxes and get some curtains and blinds on the windows. We stuffed our underwear and pajamas in the dresser drawers and called it quits.

We piled all the empty boxes together and threw them down the steps one after the other. Of course, Aunt Dilly heard the commotion and came tearing around the house. She looked really rattled. Her straight brown hair was coming loose from her bun, and wisps of it were hanging in her face. She had on an ugly, old, flowered, cotton dress that was belted and hiked up on both sides.

"Didja git all them beds made?" she yelled.

Aunt Dilly nearly always yelled. I often wondered later on if maybe she couldn't hear very well and assumed no one else could.

"Yep," I answered. "All but Joe and Alvin's. There was too much stuff on it. We didn't know what to do with it, so we just left it alone."

She made us help her carry lots of boxes in the house. And she set about arranging things in some of the rooms. Joe and Alvin had fixed a bed for Mommy in the front room just off the hall. Dickie would sleep with Mommy as he had ever since he was born. Most of Aunt Dilly's furniture had been spoiled by the mud and had to be thrown away, but her bedroom furniture was not damaged. It was just a logical thing that they would move in with us until they could get on their feet. Uncle Arlie was going around everywhere that he heard about job openings trying to find something to do. There was a possibility of a job in the mines in Minden where three of my uncles and aunts lived. He was going to go down there as soon as we got things settled in this new house.

Aunt Dilly kept us busy till Grandma sent Bertie down to tell us to come up and eat dinner. We trotted up the cement steps and down the alley to Grandma's. She had a big bowl of dumplings and gravy setting in the middle of the big round table. There was a platter of fried chicken and a bowl of peas. She was taking the pan of big brown biscuits out of the oven when we got there. Boy, everything looked and smelled so delicious. We dug in, and it was just as good as it looked. There was a lot of talking and laughing till we got our mouths full, then everything got pretty quiet. We filled Grandma in on our progress and assured her that we would be having supper in our own house. She didn't say so, but I bet she was glad. We helped her stack up the dishes and carry them to the kitchen. She always left the remaining food on the table and covered it with a tablecloth. There wasn't any food left this time. We cleaned it up.

We left and went back down to our house and helped Aunt Dilly finish putting things away. She had put a pot of pinto beans on the stove, and they were simmering and starting to fill the house with a good smell. Somehow just the familiar aroma of those beans cooking gave me a good, warm feeling and made this house seem more like home and not so foreboding. With most of the furniture in place, it seemed cozier than it had early in the morning when it was empty.

We knew that as soon as Mommy came home, she and Aunt Dilly would start washing clothes. We got the Maytag wringer washer ready and set two big zinc tubs on old wooden chairs that didn't have any backs on them. As soon as mommy came home, she filled the washer with hot water from the spigot for the first time. We all just stood around and gaped at the amazing, hot, steaming water actually coming out of a spigot. No more heating big pans of water on the stove. It was quite a long time until we got used to a gas stove and water heater. Natural gas was cheap, and we also had gas heaters to keep us warm. I didn't think much about it at the time, but I have since wondered why we would use gas for everything when West Virginia was a coal state. Some things just don't make sense. We did have back-to-back fireplaces in the living room and the front bedroom.

Joe and Alvin helped Aunt Dilly string wash lines criss-crossing in the dining room, kitchen and some on each end of the back porch. Then they went upstairs and moved all the stuff off their bed, and Aunt Dilly put sheets and blankets on it. Mommy always washed several loads of clothes, and after the supper dishes were put away, she hung them on the lines to dry overnight.

She got up early every morning, washed more clothes, took the ones down that she had hung up the night before, sprinkled them and hung up the ones she had just finished washing. Then she would walk about 12 blocks to the sewing factory and work all day.

As long as Aunt Dilly lived with us, she did most of the ironing. After they moved to Minden, Charlotte and I would come home from school and start to iron. Then we could take the laundry home before the stores closed to get food for the next day and sometimes for the same day. As soon as Mommy came home, she started ironing the shirts and dresses. This had been the pattern of our lives for as long as I could remember. It's called a hand-to-mouth existence. The rainy weather and the mud slide had put a temporary hold on Mommy's laundry business, but things soon got back on target. The rain had stopped, and we were now in a place where we could start a new life.

As I looked around the table while Mommy was saying grace, I suddenly didn't feel sad anymore. Everything was so different, but it seemed OK now. There were 10 of us seated around the big wooden table, nine with their heads bowed and their eyes closed. There was big bowl of pinto beans and a platter of corn bread, and it just felt right. Uncle Arlie, Aunt Dilly and Marie had been with us off and on, so it was just fitting that they were there now. They really didn't have any place to go. Aunt Dilly was a big help to Mommy, doing the housework and looking after us wild Indians. Alvin and Joe had been part of our family for so long that it just seemed natural, too. Then there were my Mommy, Charlotte, Bertie and little sweet Dickie. I shut my eyes just as Mommy said "amen" and opened them just as quickly. So much for our first day in the house on 11th Avenue.

CHAPTER *2*

Bozo

We had been living down on 11th Avenue for about a year.
Mommy had gone to her Sunday school teacher's house,
which was about a block down toward the West End. They
were having their monthly class meeting, and Mommy told me
to bring some cupcakes down at 8:30 p.m. She had just iced
them before she left, but she had some other stuff to carry.
Since it wasn't far, she figured I could just bring them down.
She had them all lined up in a box lid on the kitchen table.

There were three houses in a row going up the right side
of the hill. We lived in the middle one. Deeds lived in the
house toward the street, and Lillys lived in the upper one.
There was a wide grassy yard out front, and on the opposite

side of the yard were three more houses lined up just like ours. Cheethams lived in the top one, and I can't remember who lived in the other two. There were circles of flower gardens planted down the middle of the yard. There was a series of cement steps, then a platform at each house. At the bottom of the steps and the yard was a high wall, about six or seven feet high. Temple Street ran along the wall. All the houses were built up off the street and had long rows of cement steps in front.

I got the cupcakes off the kitchen table and went out the front door. I went down the steps from our house to the platform at Deeds, then down a longer set of steps to the main street. I turned to the right toward the West End and suddenly, without warning, Billy Joe Cheetham's German Shepherd dog, Bozo, came tearing down the avenue and took a flying leap over the wall. He knocked me off my feet and sent the cupcakes flying through the air. I landed on my butt, and Bozo jumped on me and began snarling and barking and biting my face and neck. I was screaming and trying to fight him off. I was backing up like a crab and the dog just kept attacking me. He bit me in my eyebrows, my cheek, my neck and my arms and hands. I was hysterical by this time and was a screaming bloody mess.

Billy Joe heard the commotion and ran down the avenue and jumped over the wall. He was yelling at Bozo, but the dog just ignored him. Billy Joe got him by the collar and tried to pull him off me, but the dog just persisted with the viscous attack. I've been told that by this time that one-half the neighborhood was out of their houses and gathered around. The chief of police, who lived across the street, came running over. He ordered Billy Joe to get the dog off me. When he saw that the dog was not responding, he shot him in the neck. The dog slumped dead weight over my body, gave a gasp and his head lolled over to one side. I was still doing the crab crawl and screaming at the top of my lungs. Now there was a big dead dog lying on top of me, and his blood was oozing out and mingling with mine.

I don't know to this day who picked me up and took me to the hospital. They patched me up, gave me some medicine and sent me home. I had stitches in my eyebrow, my cheek and my lip. There were some bites and scratches on both my hands and arms. I had hysterical fits of crying for weeks after the incident. And I woke up at night in a cold sweat, screaming. I wasn't in a lot of pain, but I was so traumatized by the entire incident.

No one could figure out what triggered Bozo to attack me. He was not considered a mean dog and had never bothered anyone before. I had never been afraid of him. They had lived neighbors to us for as long as we had lived on 11th Avenue. I had never teased him, and he was always around whenever Billy Joe was. They determined he was about 5 years old, and when they checked him, he didn't have rabies. Someone said there might have been something in the cupcakes that set him off. I'll never know, but I have been deathly afraid of dogs ever since. I will avoid them whenever I can. I will cross the street rather than go past a dog, even if it's on a leash, behind a fence or tied up. I bet I've heard the phrase, "He won't hurt you; he's friendly" 100 times. Well, Bozo was friendly too, but he hurt me.

I have lost a lot of friends over their dog. People like their dogs a lot better than they do me. Folks who love dogs can't understand my attitude, but I just can't help it. I guess you could say I have a phobia where dogs are concerned. Today probably a kid who was attacked by a dog could get some kind of counseling and work through the fear, but there was no such thing available for me at that time. I would rather face a lion or a tiger than a dog — even a little one.

CHAPTER *3*

My First Date

My first date was a total disaster. It was my 13th birthday, and I had a party. It was a bitter cold night on Dec. 21, 1939, but there was a nice big fire burning in the fireplace. We had the couch pulled up in front of the fire and about 18 or 20 kids were sitting on the floor, on the couch and on chairs all as close as they could get to the warmth of the fire. We sang a lot of Christmas carols and played a lot of kissin' games. We played Spin the Bottle, Spotlight and Post Office, and I think everyone had a good time.

I opened my gifts, and we had ice cream and cake. Mommy always managed somehow to make sure we had a cake with

Anna Jean, age 11

candles on it and some ice cream for our birthdays.

After the party was over, we were all just milling around laughing and talking. One by one the kids were leaving. Well, this one boy, Russell Morgan, he sidled up to me and quietly asked me if I would go to the movies with him.

That's what he said, "Anna Jean, will you go to the movies with me?"

Wow! I wasn't sure what I was supposed to do or say. I'm pretty sure I turned a bright red. I couldn't even look at him.

I mumbled, "Yeah, I guess so."

I don't remember exactly what I did after that, but everyone went home except Russell. We moved the couch and chairs back where they belonged and helped Mommy straighten up the living room. I asked her if I could go to the movies with Russell. She gave me a sly grin and said, "Yes. Be home by 9:30."

We put on our coats, hats, gloves and boots and went outside. It had snowed a couple of days before, but the walks were clear. We went down the steps and down to the sidewalk below. Neither one of us said anything. We just walked along in an awkward silence. Huh, some date! We walked along for about a block when Russell reached over and took hold of my hand. I didn't pull away, but it felt strange to be walking down the street holding hands with a boy, Russell Morgan at that.

Russell was a little, short guy with freckles. Not the best looking fellow in the world, but then Hollywood hadn't discovered me yet either. We had been in the same grade since first grade. He lived right down below me on the corner of Temple Street and 11th Avenue. We had played together for years, studied together and walked home along with a bunch of kids who lived out our way. For some reason, this was different, and we were both embarrassed and ill at ease.

I finally got my tongue and asked him, "Did you have a good time at the party?"

"It was OK," he said.

I don't remember what we talked about for the rest of the way to the Masonic Theater. I remember my hand got sweaty, and I wanted to let go of his. But I was afraid it would make him mad, so I didn't. When we got to the corner of Fifth Avenue, he loosened his grip, and we were finally separated.

Whew, what a relief. I was afraid we would go all the way through town hooked together, but we didn't.

We went past the high school and crossed the street to the theater. We walked up to the cashier's window. Russell pushed a dime through the opening in the glass and got a ticket — one ticket.

He stepped back beside me, and we just stood there looking at each other.

"Well?" he said.

"Well, what?" I asked him.

"Well, get your ticket," he answered.

I was so embarrassed I wanted to drop dead right there on the spot.

"I don't have a dime," I whispered hoarsely.

I was looking down at my feet. I had a good notion to just turn around and start running home, but for some reason, I just stood there. I never felt so stupid and mad in my life.

"I don't have another one either," he said.

We stood there looking at each other for a few seconds. He turned around, walked over to the window and asked the lady to give him his dime back. He took my hand, and we walked over next door to Fred Maddy's. That was a place where kids hung out after school and at lunchtime. They also sold magazines, cigarettes, over-the-counter medicine and other stuff I can't remember. We went to the counter, and Russell ordered two Cokes. We walked over to a booth and just sat there quietly sipping our Cokes. Finally Russell broke the ice.

"Why did you come along if you didn't have a dime?" he asked me.

I didn't want to talk about it, so I mumbled something. I was too embarrassed.

"What?" he whispered. "I can't hear you."

I leaned across the table and hissed, "How come you asked me if you wasn't going to pay my way?"

"Are you nuts?" he whispered back. "I never said I was going to pay your way to the movies. I just asked you if you wanted to go with me."

I was so darned mad by this time that I swigged the last of my Coke, got up and practically ran out the door. I started walking down the street toward home. The faster I walked, the madder I got. About the middle of the block I heard Russell calling me. He was running along behind me trying to catch up. I wasn't about to slow down. At that particular moment I wanted nothing to do with that dumb jerk. He finally caught up with me and started walking along beside me.

"What's the matter?" he asked me breathlessly. "What did I do that's so terrible?"

I came to a stop so abruptly that he was several steps ahead of me by the time he realized that I had stopped.

"What did you do?" I yelled at him. "What did you do? You just made a fool out of me; that's what you did. I can't believe you're that dumb, Russell Morgan. You go to the same school as I do, and you've been going to the same movies that I have since we were little kids. Ain't you learned nothing? Don't you know that when a boy asks a girl out on a date, he pays her way to the movies?"

"This ain't no date," he yelled back at me. I just wanted you to go to the movies with me."

"That's called a date, dummy, whether you like it or not; and you had no right to let me think you were actually going to take me to the movies."

I was trying not to let him see that I was on the verge of tears. I went over and sat down on the steps of the high school. Russell came over and sat down about three feet from me. It was pretty awkward, but neither one of us knew what to do next.

Finally he stood up and said, "Come on, Anna Jean. Let's go home."

I got up, and we started walking toward the West End.

"I'm really sorry," he offered. "I didn't mean for things to turn out like this. I just wanted us to go to the movies together. I guess you won't have nothing to do with me from now on, will you?"

I didn't answer. I didn't want to talk to him anymore. I was all mixed up and mad and hurt. I just wanted to get home and put an end to this awful evening. We walked along in silence for about a block. Finally I moved over closer to him and asked, "Russell, why did you ask me to go to the movies with you in the first place?"

He didn't answer right away, and then he said so quietly that I could hardly hear him, "'Cause I like you."

Shucks. Now what was I supposed to do? Poor Russell, he really didn't know any better. I'd always liked Russell. We'd always had fun together, but I wasn't sure I liked the turn things were taking.

"OK, Russell, let's just forget this whole thing. From now on, we'll still be friends, but you won't ever ask me to go to the movies with you. We'll just go to the movies together. That way we'll both know we're each going to pay our own way."

We were walking along as we talked. Russell reached over, took my arm and stopped me.

"That's a good idea. Umm, you're not mad at me anymore?" He sounded relieved. I really felt sorry for him. My mad was all gone.

"Naw. I'm not mad anymore," I whispered.

Neither one of us said much as we walked the rest of the way home. When we got to my house, we went in. There was still a good fire in the fireplace, so we took off our winter garb and flopped down on the couch. Mommy heard us and came in. She gave us a funny look.

"That must have been a real short movie; it's only 8:15."

Russell and I looked at each other. Then we both started laughing.

"We decided not to go. We didn't think we would like the movie, so we just had a Coke at Fred's and came home."

We sat on the couch for about an hour. We talked about my party, about Christmas, about school. We covered just about every subject we could think of, but we never mentioned the movie we didn't see. About 9:30 Russell got ready to go home. I went to the door with him, and he kissed me good night.

"I'm glad you're not mad at me," he whispered in my ear. "Can I come up tomorrow?"

"OK," I said. "Maybe we can go to the movies together."

He gave me a little grin and said, "It's a date."

We both burst out laughing at our little joke. And that's how it was for about a year. We went together. We went to the movies about once a week, but he never asked me to go to the movies with him. We just went to the movies together. I paid my way, and he paid his. But I never went anywhere again without at least a dime in my pocket.

CHAPTER *4*

Small Towns

We never did go very far up the social ladder, but every time Mommy moved us she got a little farther out of the deep hole she had fallen into when she fell in love with and married Daddy.

In a little town there is what is called a "small town mindset." If you weren't born there, you are never going to be a native. If you don't have money, you are doomed to stay at the bottom of the heap. Even your name could cause aversion for absolutely no other reason than the name itself. You could never outlive your name. The only way to make it in a small town is to get the heck out of the small town.

Small towns can really do a number on you if you let them. Mommy refused to succumb to them. She held her head high and walked like she was royalty. Some of the narrow-minded, bigoted folks resented her attitude and thought she was "puttin' on airs" or "being snooty." Some (most) folks admired her and loved her because of or despite it. The funny thing was, she wasn't doing anything except being herself. That's just who she was. She wasn't haughty or arrogant. She was just optimistic and confident. No matter how many low blows or raw deals life handed her, or how often she was knocked down, she got right back up, climbed to where she had been before and reached for yet another plateau.

There's a lot of good about a small town, too. For one thing, everybody knows everybody and though most of them are a bit on the nosy side, this can sometimes be a good thing. When trouble comes to a family, the whole town soon knows about it and rallies around to help. Hinton was a delightful little town to grow up in. I had a glorious childhood and wouldn't change a moment of it.

There were a lot of churches in Hinton; nearly everybody went to church. There were a lot of religious folks in town, but not all of them were really true Christians. There are a lot of reasons why most people go to church.

Number one, it's Sunday; that's the day you're supposed to go to church. That is unless you are a Seventh Day Adventist; then you go on Saturday.

Number two, it's a habit. Your mom and dad probably went to church and made you go when you were growing up, so now you feel guilty if you don't go.

Number three, there are a lot of people in church, so you get to see people and have fun. It's a social thing, some

Temple Street in Hinton, W.V.

place to go, something to do. It's good for your reputation to say what church you belong to, especially if you're applying for a job.

Number four, you get to dress up in your Sunday best and show off your good clothes. OK, now what's wrong with this picture? What should be the main reason for going to church? To worship God, of course.

Oh, that gets stuck in there someplace, but it's not a priority with most folks; it's an afterthought. Of course, this is not only true of small towns; it's just that it's more likely to be acceptable where everybody knows everybody else. It just wouldn't do not to go to church. Everybody would think something was wrong with you.

We went to the First Christian Church on Seventh Avenue. Preacher Atkins was a good man. He was a true Christian, not just a churchgoer. I don't know what denomination that church was. Just Christians was all I ever heard us called, not Catholics or Presbyterians or Methodists or Baptists or Episcopalians or Lutherans. Just Christians. Very misleading name, because although there were some mighty good people in that church, by no stretch of the imagination could they all be called Christians, same as any other church.

I remember one Saturday I went to work for a woman who was an outstanding member of our church. I worked from 7 in the morning till 7 that night. I scrubbed floors, changed both beds, washed the sheets on a wringer washer, hung them out, took them in and ironed them, (yes, in those days people ironed their sheets and pillowcases). I washed windows, swept and dusted the whole two-story house, cleaned the kitchen floor and waxed it and scrubbed the front porch. She gave me a quarter. I was so mad, I could hardly talk. When I got home and showed Mommy my quarter, she took me by the arm, and we marched right down to Mrs. Blankety Blank's house. Mommy knocked on the door, and when she opened it, Mommy reached out and placed the quarter in her hand.

"Here," she said firmly but politely, "is your quarter back. Don't ever insult my daughter again by working her for 12 hours and handing her a measly quarter. Good day."

Mommy was still holding me firmly by the arm. She turned around, and we marched right off that porch, leaving Mrs. Tightwad standing there with her mouth open. Mommy was the Sunday school teacher, and on Sunday morning she taught the lesson about a fair-day's pay for a fair-day's work. She didn't call any names or mention the cleaning incident nor was she snide or condemning. But she got her point across. I found this out later when I overheard some of the women in the class discussing the lesson, and I knew the point had been made. I never worked for that lady again. Mommy gave me a quarter.

Another thing about small towns — almost everybody has a front porch. Usually there is a main street, and it stretches the entire length of the town. There may or may not be a couple of parallel streets, and at every block is an avenue or side street. The main street in Hinton was called Temple Street, below was Summers Street and above was Ballangee Street. Temple Street started at the bridge at the East End of town and ran all the way out to the West End toward Brooks. We lived on 11th Avenue, and it was quite a walk downtown. Everybody had a front porch, and there was somebody sitting on all those porches in the summer time. All the houses on our side of the street were way up off the sidewalk and had a row of cement steps going up to the porches. People on the porches could look down and see anybody who went by, but it was difficult to see up and over the banisters.

I used to hate to go past some of these houses because I knew some of the nosy old women were just waiting to scrutinize and gossip about any and everything anyone did and the way they looked. Lots of times I would go up and walk down through the alley past Grandma Bennett's just so I wouldn't have to walk past certain houses.

Another place I hated to walk past was the corner of the Big Four Drug Store. There were steps going down the side of the building on Temple Street and an iron railing across the steps. There was always a group of young guys sitting on that rail just ogling everyone who went past. They even

Two of the "rail sitters,"
Bob Evans (left) and K.D. Foster.

formed a club called "The Rail Sitters" and were very proud of themselves. Of course, they would make faces and weird gestures. They often whistled, made comments and other strange noises. I guess those fellows had an opinion of just about everybody in town, as sooner or later everyone would go past that corner. I was embarrassed by the attention when I went past but secretly just a little flattered by the whistles. There were regulars, and I think some of them spent so much time on the rail "watchin' all the girls go by" that they didn't have much time to get a life.

For every unsavory character in town, there were dozens of fine, friendly and sincere individuals who worked diligently to make the world a better place. Hinton was no exception. There were many dedicated teachers, preachers, doctors, merchants, politicians and just plain ordinary good folks who made up the kaleidoscope of the small town.

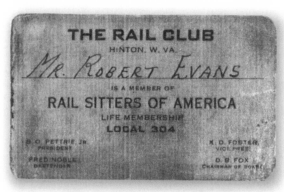

The "rail sitters" even had
membership cards made up.

My Uncle Carl was the manager of a Community Center on Temple Street, and I loved to go there. There was a loom, and anybody could go in and sit at the loom and work on a rug. It had foot pedals, and you would alternate with ups and downs and feed the strings through to the other side with a wooden thing. I think it was called a shuttle. There was something that you pulled across the whole thing, and it pushed the threads together and made the pattern. Carl would keep watch and stop when the rug got long enough. Then he'd roll the whole thing for about six or eight inches, and we'd start another one. When the thread got to the end, he would take the whole thing off and cut the rugs apart. We'd sit around and tie the ends. I don't know what they did with the rugs. I just liked to work on them.

There were all kinds of crafts in the building like painting and drawing pictures. People learned to knit and crochet and make quilts. There was carpentry and woodworking. There was some simple stuff for little kids, like making macaroni jewelry and painting it. Also there were lots of crafts using buttons, scraps of material or leaves, twigs and wood. There were lots of books and tables where you could sit and read. You could write letters or do your lessons. It was a nice, friendly place, and I have no idea why it was eventually closed down.

One of my most favorite spots in town was the Ritz Theater on Ballangee Street. I managed to get there every Saturday for the cowboy show. When I was little, I'd go when it opened at 11 a.m. and stay till Mommy came and made me go home usually about suppertime. Grandma Bennett always took one or two of us kids on Wednesday night. That was when they had a drawing and somebody would win a prize. I can't remember exactly what the prizes were, but the theater was always packed on Wednesday nights. They stopped the show at intermission, and someone played the piano at the end of the stage. They rolled a big pot out to the middle and drew a name out. It was a very exciting time. When I was a teenager, I went a lot with my boyfriend. We would get a hot dog, popcorn and a Coke at Mathew's concession stand next to the theater. We sat in the back row and ate and enjoyed the movie. That was a big date.

There was a skating rink. Once in a while there were some school dances, and everyone went to them. Of course, the football games were the pinnacle of social activity during the school year. There were some roadhouses up the river, but I never went. For one thing, nobody I knew had a car, and they were considered a little too wild for me. They sold alcohol, and Mommy would have tanned my butt if she ever heard that I had been to one of them.

CHAPTER 5

Central Burns

Several of us kids were sleigh riding down the hill from Ballangee Street to Temple Street one evening. It was bitter cold and had snowed for several days. The roads were good and slippery. We had to go past the Central School, which was between Temple and Ballangee.

After awhile, as we were pulling our sleds back up the street, someone whispered, "Look, there is some smoke coming out of the basement windows of the Central School house."

"Wow," someone said, "maybe the school house is on fire, and it'll burn down. We won't have to go to school no more."

"Yeah," a kid replied, "wouldn't that be wonderful?"

Some smart aleck had to go and say, "Maybe we ought to tell somebody."

"Yeah, well, who're we gonna tell?" another kid chimed in. "Maybe it ain't on fire at all. Maybe somebody's just burning something down there."

"Let's go up to the top of the hill, and when we come back down we can see if it really is a fire," some wise and wonderful child offered.

This seemed to make sense to everyone, so we trudged up the street. Just as we got to Ballangee Street, we saw Logan Cox, the janitor, turn around and wave at us. All of a sudden he started running back down to the school. He was yelling that there was smoke and that we had better get back down the hill. We all turned and started sliding down, one after the other on our sleds. When we got to the bottom, we all jumped off our sleds and walked over to the sidewalk and stared at the basement windows of the school. Thick smoke was pouring out of several of the windows, and we could see flames flickering through the smoke. There was no doubt now in anyone's mind that there was indeed a fire. We all looked at each other for a couple of seconds, and leaving our sleds on the sidewalk, we started running down Temple Street to Fred Maddy's. That was a soda fountain where the school kids hung out. We burst in and all started babbling at once.

Fred calmed us down enough so that he could understand what we were trying to tell him. He called the fire company and explained that the schoolhouse was on fire. Logan had already called, and the fire company was on the way. We ran back outside, but we couldn't see anything from this side of the building. We hurried down Temple Street to the corner of Fifth Avenue. We could see that flames were leaping out of the basement windows, and there was smoke coming out of some of the first floor windows. A crowd was gathering as people began to notice the smoke and realized there was a fire in the schoolhouse. Pretty soon the fire sirens started screaming through the cold winter night. Just the sound of the sirens was enough to create an atmosphere of excitement. Men were running toward the schoolhouse from all directions. Several of them were without coats even though it was a very cold night. I learned later that the temperature was several degrees below zero. A couple of men went toward the burning building but were forced back by the intense heat. The building was quickly becoming engulfed in flames, and it was apparent that something was causing the rapid exhilaration of the fire.

We kids went across the street where we had been sleigh riding. We hunched together and whispered stuff about maybe we should have told somebody sooner.

"I knew we should have told somebody right away," piped up the smart aleck, who had said those very words earlier. No one wanted to hear him rub it in. We were all feeling guilty and miserable enough. It was sort of like we were somehow responsible because after all, we did notice the smoke and could have and should have alerted some one right away.

"Gee, I hope they don't think we started it," someone muttered.

It seemed an eternity until the fire company arrived, but actually I think it was only about eight or 10 minutes. The men jumped down from the truck and began hooking the hoses up to the fire hydrants. Everyone was yelling and barking out orders. Some of the men who were there early started herding the crowd back from the premises, so the firemen could do their job. I sneaked through the crowd and got my sled. I could feel the heat from the fire now, as the entire building was a raging inferno. I went across the street and sat down on my sled. But then I couldn't see the firemen, so I got up and stood up on my sled. Wow! What a sight. The firemen were shooting big streams of water on the building, but it didn't do one bit of good. That building just burned and burned and burned. I don't remember if any other fire companies were there or not, but I guess they probably were. There was so much commotion and so many people milling around, it was real chaos. Nobody wanted to go home, so the whole town just stood around and watched. People were trying to squeeze through the throng to get a better look. There was a lot of crying and talking. Everyone was trying to speculate on how the fire might have been started. Some thought that it might have been set on purpose. Some thought that maybe the furnace blew up. The only positive thing anyone had to say was that it was just a good thing the fire happened in the evening instead of during the day when school was in progress.

We must have stood around for a couple of hours, just watching the school building burn. I remember it was still burning but not as fiercely when Mommy found me and made us all go home. We wanted to stay, but Mommy said she had to go to work in the morning and needed some rest. It was close to midnight till we all got home and settled down for the night. I was sure I wasn't going to sleep a wink, but after Charlotte and I whispered for awhile, the

Hinton High School

next thing I knew it was morning. The sun was streaming through the window. I lay there for awhile and thought about the previous night. I climbed out of bed and ran downstairs. Our room upstairs was not heated, and the floor and steps were icy cold. The living room was toasty warm, and there was no one around. The clock on the kitchen wall had 10:30. Mommy had left a note on the kitchen table informing us that there was no school today. Duh, no kidding. She gave each of us instructions on how to behave and some chores to do. I drank some coffee and ate a biscuit with butter and jelly. I went back upstairs and put my clothes on. It was too cold in the bathroom, so I didn't bother to wash up. I just brushed my teeth, combed my hair and went back downstairs. I added my two cents to Mommy's note telling anyone who was interested that I was going downtown to check on the high school fire.

I put on my coat, hat, boots and gloves and went outside. Brrr! It was really cold. We didn't have a thermometer, but I didn't need one to tell me it was a cold, cold day. I ran down the steps and across the street to where Mary Grace and Frances lived. They were my closest friends, not only in distance, but we had been friends since we were very little. Mary Grace had lived just below us on Ninth Avenue and had moved down to Temple Street about a year before we did. Frances had moved to Hinton a couple of years before and had blended in with our bunch. They shared a double house. I yelled from the porch and almost immediately Frances poked her head out the door of the apartment on the right.

"What's up?" she asked. "Come on in out of the cold."

"OK," I said, "wait till I get Mary Grace."

"She's in here," Frances answered. "Get in quick, so I don't have to hold the door open so long."

I slipped past her into the living room, and she quickly shut the door.

I didn't see Mary Grace, but before I could ask, Frances informed me that she was in the bathroom.

"She'll be out in a minute," Frances grinned.

Frances' living room was almost identical to Mary Grace's. Both took piano lessons and had a piano at the far end of the room. There was a gray frieze davenport along the middle wall. There was a window on the right side of the room with a desk on one side and a chair that matched the davenport on the other side There were a couple of small tables with lamps on them beside the couch and chair.

Mary Grace came through the archway with a silly grin on her face.

"I'm goin' downtown to see the schoolhouse," I said, "Wanna come along?"

"Sure," both girls answered in unison and went to get their coats and boots.

We went down the street at a pretty brisk pace because it was so cold, and we were anxious to see the ruins of the school. We talked breathlessly about the fire; how it started and what was going to happen now that there wasn't any high school. We were hoping there wouldn't be any school — at least for awhile.

When we got to the corner of Fourth Avenue and crossed the street, we stopped dead in our tracks. Where the schoolhouse had been, there now stood a gorgeous massive ice castle. It looked like something out of a fairy tale. During the night the water that the firemen had poured into and on the building to try to extinguish the fire had frozen in solid sheets of icicles, which hung like a gossamer drapery over the entire building. It was the most breathtaking sight I had ever seen in my short life. We weren't the only observers of this unique and unusual phenomenon. The sidewalks were lined on all sides with onlookers who were just as awestruck as we were. A few people were taking pictures, and I later learned that earlier that morning the newspaper photographers had been there also.

After the tragic and awesome events of the day before, came the stark reality of the present. No school building, so no school! That was our dream, but it turned into a nightmare, at least for the kids. The school board members already had their heads together and were busy cooking up a scheme to ensure all of us little heathens would continue our education as swiftly and effectively as possible. They scoured the town for available space that would be suitable, if not necessarily the most desirable, to temporarily conduct classes. Of course there was nothing any of us could do but wait. It was not long before the announcement was made by word of mouth and in the daily newspaper that school would resume on a regular basis the following week. Locations and schedules were posted all over town as well as each day in the newspaper. Classes were held in the library, band room, home economics building and just about anywhere there was usable space.

A thorough investigation revealed that the furnace had overheated and creosote, which had built up in the chimney, caused the fire. There was so much paper and wooden furniture that it was fueled in a short time to an uncontrollable raging inferno.

It was impossible to even attempt to tear down the remains of the old building because of the extremely cold temperature and the enormity of the ice formation on the remaining structure. It was determined that at the earliest thaw, the demolition and construction would begin. A 10-room, two-story brick building was constructed early in the spring. So, alas, our dreams of a long vacation literally went up in smoke.

CHAPTER 6

Teachers

I have often tried to figure out why I can remember some of my teachers so vividly, and others I can't remember their names or what they looked like.

I remember Mrs. Kennedy, my fourth-grade teacher. She was skinny with blond, curly hair cut in sort of a bob. I guess she was pretty, at least she was to me. She was always friendly and full of energy. She sent away for anything she could get for free. She always had little, special treats for the kids who did their lessons correctly and on time. She gave each of us a flat, wooden box filled with dirt in the springtime and flower seeds to plant in them. We had to water our little garden and fill out a report every week on its progress. Our gardens had little wooden sticks in them with our names on them, so we could tell which one was ours. Mine didn't do too well, so I traded every weekend with someone whose garden was thriving. All I had to do was switch the name sticks. I wound up at the beginning of summer vacation with a very healthy plant.

Mrs. Kennedy was the teacher who dreamed up the circus parade art project. We worked an hour a day for a whole year making animals, cages, clowns and all the other strange and unusual things that made a circus so magical and wonderful. We used yards and yards of brown butcher paper and lots and lots of flour paste to put together what I remember as a real masterpiece. The only thing I can't remember about Mrs. Kennedy is what she taught. It must have been something because I went from fourth grade to fifth grade without a hitch.

I remember Mr. Allen, my seventh-grade teacher. He was a little short man with brown wavy hair and full lips and was nearly always grinning. He was a good teacher and very friendly with everyone. He taught either United States or World History, and I wasn't the least bit interested in history of any kind. The only time I had a run in with him was over chewing gum in class. I was always chewing gum, and he was always making me get rid of it. One day he told me if I intended to chew gum in class, I should just bring enough for everyone, and we'd all chew gum. I'm sorry. This was not an intelligent way to handle a smart aleck. I knew he was being sarcastic, but the next day I calmly went from desk to desk and handed a stick of gum to everyone. Nobody touched the gum, and gradually the room got very quiet. That's the loudest silence I've ever heard.

One of Anna Jean's elementary classes.
She is in the front row, second from left.

Mr. Allen picked up a yardstick from the blackboard and ordered me to come up to the front of the room. When I walked toward him, I could see that he was really mad. He had his lips shut tightly, and his eyes had a funny look in them. As I approached him, he got me by the arm and raised the yardstick and brought it down with considerable force. I reacted instinctively. I reached out and took hold of the yardstick, and it broke in half. This made him madder and scared me half to death, but he didn't let go of my arm. He raised his arm up and was going to hit me with the half of a yardstick. Again I reached out just as his hand was coming down and grabbed hold of the broken end of the yardstick. It broke again. Now he was really mad, and I was afraid he was going to kill me. He raised his hand up holding the stub of yardstick to finish me off, I guess. I let out a bloodcurdling scream, which made everyone jump and caused him to loosen his hold on my arm just as he was about to clobber me with his fist. I grabbed his wrist and wrenched free from his hold on me and went tearing out the door, down to the principal's office.

I ran in the office without knocking, which was a no no. I was bawling and blubbering to Mr. Withers that Mr. Allen was trying to hit me. There was a secretary in the office, and they made me sit down. I tried to tell them what had happened, but of course, I acted like I didn't know what had set him off. I neglected to explain about the little chewing gum escapade. From my version, I was a totally innocent victim of an enraged madman.

Mr. Allen was summoned to the office, and I cowered in the chair and stared at the floor while he told his version of what had happened. I had no doubt that the proper authorities would believe him. To my amazement, he was reprimanded for trying to use corporal punishment on a young lady. Me? A lady? This was a new twist. I was given a lecture about the proper way to conduct myself in classrooms and ordered to show respect for my teacher, or I would be suspended. Mr. Allen was warned about using force on students. Wow! All this over a little stick of gum — well, maybe more than one little stick of gum.

When I went back to class, it was pretty quiet. Everyone knew what had happened in the classroom, but they didn't know what had transpired in the principal's office. I have to admit that although I wasn't a perfect angel after that, I was a bit leery about trying to be cute in Mr. Allen's class. Of course, everyone in the whole school heard about the incident, and it was blown all out of proportion. The truth got lost somewhere as the tale traveled from mouth to mouth, and facts got distorted.

Another teacher who made quite an indelible mark in my memory was Ada Thompson. Now there was a teacher. She taught English Literature, and she taught from the heart. She lived and breathed her classes. I can see her yet, a feisty little woman with dark curly hair and an incredible enthusiasm. She was so animated that she made the stories and poems come to life. She knew them all by heart. And she marched across the room, she ran across the room, she hung her head, she moaned and groaned, she whispered, she shouted, she laughed, she cried, she made faces. Whatever the story called for, she acted it out. I can still see her reciting my favorite poem, *The Highwayman*. Her voice would lower, and she would hunch over and whisper whenever there was a tender or suspenseful moment. Then she would stand erect, throw her head back and thrust her body and arm forward and literally march across the room.

"Back he spurred like a madman shrieking a curse to the sky, his pistol butts afore him, his rapier brandished high. And they shot him down on the highway, down like a dog on the highway and he died like a dog on the highway, drenched in his own red blood."

She was practically lying dead on the floor before us. I can still recite most of that poem, along with others she drilled into my mind.

She was also the Girl Scout leader and often took us camping and river rafting.

Some things she wasn't too bright about, though. For instance, her idea of punishing a boy was to make him sit in the seat with a girl. Now this was in seventh grade, and of course, we were all just beginning to appreciate the opposite sex. So this fell flat as punishment. One day she made this guy come over and sit with me. We thought it was pretty funny, and we had our heads together whispering and giggling. She said if we were going to neck, we could go out in the hall and do it. She meant to embarrass us, but we just got up and started out the door. By golly, she got ticked and ordered us back in the room. She made us both stay for an hour after school and write some kind of a dumb essay on how to behave in school.

Then there was Eleanor Meadows. She taught English. She was like a princess with big brown eyes, a lovely complexion and very dark wavy hair. She was a petite woman who seemed so frail and dainty that we were afraid to do or say anything that would upset her. She was by far the prettiest teacher we had. She was very young, and I think we had her the first year she got out of college and began her teaching career. All the guys had a crush on her, and the girls wanted to get in and stay in her good graces. She was a good teacher, too. She had a way of making each of us feel special. That's a real gift, and I'm not sure she even knew just how effective she was. She even taught me. Because of her and Ada Thompson I developed a deep love for and interest in literature and English that I might not have with other teachers.

There were some teachers I remember because they were so mean and hateful. I'd rather not call them by name, but I guess they're all dead by now, so it doesn't matter. Some

Anna Jean (second row, second from right) with her seventh grade class.

people are just not cut out to be teachers. They do an injustice to a whole generation of students by getting into and staying in a profession, which is so vital to society, and not doing a decent job.

One woman, in particular, Miss Dakum, should have been tarred and feathered. She was snotty, deceitful and downright sadistic in some of her classroom requirements. I had sense enough to steer clear of her and toe the line, but she rode me anyway. Now you're probably thinking if she had me under control, she must have been a heck of a good teacher and disciplinarian.

Well, maybe so, but I remember some of the awful things she did to some of the other poor kids, and it makes me want to puke even now. Miss Dakum was a real snob and was always catering to the kids if their parents were a little influential or had some money. Now that's OK to a degree, and it's just human nature to cozy up to certain people and have an aversion to others. But a teacher in a public school, with the assortment of sizes, shapes and colors that kids come in, should have some degree of equality in their demeanor. Well, she didn't. If a child had any kind of deviation from what her idea of perfection was, she ostracized them, humiliated them, terrified them and even threatened them. Most kids were so terrified of what her revenge or retaliation might be that they never dared to say anything negative about her.

She was jealous of every other female teacher who was the least bit attractive and even jealous of the high school girls. She was a shameless flirt and as prissy as all get out. She had all the male teachers goggle-eyed over her, as men are such asses when it comes to a pretty face. She was careful to show her Mr. Hyde side when men were around. She was a very pretty young woman with beautiful blond hair and a nice figure, but I perceived her as pure evil and could have put her God-given assets to a much better use.

The only time Mommy ever went to school to defend my shenanigans was over a notebook that was required for this course. Two of my friends and I sat up half the night copying our notebook over, so it would be accurate and neat. All the answers had been given to us during the school year. We were required to turn in the completed notebook at the end of the year. It was just a matter of turning in the notebook, and our final grade would be based on the completion and accuracy of this notebook. All three of us had identical answers, which had been given to us by the teacher during the school semester. Both of my friends got an A on their notebook, and I got a C. I was pretty upset and went home in a snit. When Mommy found out why I was upset, she checked the notebook and found no errors. The next morning she marched into the school with my notebook in her hand. She went straight to my classroom and laid the notebook on Miss Dakum's desk.

"Please show me which question is answered incorrectly," Mommy asked politely.

Miss Dakum gave her a sickening sweet smile and picked up the notebook. She flipped through it and then handed it back to Mommy.

"There are no incorrect answers in the notebook," she answered snidely.

"Was the writing legible? Was the notebook neat? Were there smudges or sloppy entries? Just what is the problem?"

Mommy shot the questions at her in rapid succession.

"Exactly what is wrong with the notebook? You gave Anna Jean a C and gave A's to each of the other girls? The girls told me that they each copied their notebook over last night, so that it would come up to your expectations. All the answers are identical and correct. Can you explain that to me, please?"

"I certainly can," she replied smugly. "Her handwriting is very poor. The other two girls have excellent handwriting. Based on the appearance, there is no comparison. I do not feel she deserves an A."

Mommy wasn't through. She calmly asked Miss Dakum, "Are you grading History or Penmanship?"

"That is beside the point," she retorted hotly. "That is the grade she deserves, and that is the grade she got."

"Thank you," Mommy politely and quietly said.

Taking the notebook with her, she turned and left the room. In less than two minutes, Mr. Withers, the principal, came into the room and told Miss Dakum to change the grade from a C to an A. She was livid with rage, but she complied. I was so glad that was the last day of school, so she didn't have a chance to get even with me. She would surely have made my life miserable if she had gotten the chance.

CHAPTER *7*

Hairpin Curves

In case you have never heard of a hairpin curve, first I might as well tell you what a hairpin is. Years ago most women had long hair and wore it twisted up or braided and piled up on top of their head. My Mommy always kept her hair long and wore a bun low on the back of her head.

In order to keep the hair secure in this fashion, hairpins were invented. They were usually made out of a thin piece of rigid wire, which was bent in the middle and curved so that the ends were even. Most were about 2 or 3 inches in length and approximately one-half inch across. Several of these hairpins could be inserted into the piled up, twisted or braided hair in a circular arrangement and thus keep the hair in place. Many variations of hairpins came and went as fashions and hair styles evolved. Some were carved of ivory, bone, shell, silver, gold, later plastic and a common style was the brown tortoise ones. Some were in the form of long-toothed combs, and many were inlaid with jewels or had intricate patterns carved on them. They also were made with the sides bent in a sort of zigzag, which made for a firmer and more permanent grip that kept them from sliding out of the hair.

So, now that you have a pretty good picture of a hairpin, keep the plain ones in mind. West Virginia is famous for its high and beautiful mountains. Building highways and railways from one city to another often meant either tunneling through these gigantic mountains or building around them. I think Highway No. 3 from Beckley to Hinton is a very good example of an extremely treacherous stretch of highway. Sheer perpendicular cliffs with deep chasms between them are typical of the landscape. Roads were literally carved out of the sides of the mountains with a sheer drop of hundreds of feet on one side and a monstrous wall of rock on the other side. Always to be revered, highways took on an even more ominous persona in the merciless fury of West Virginia winters. Heavy snowfalls and bitter cold temperatures made these highways a daredevil's delight, and the average person really was scared of the prospect of having to travel on them. Make no mistake about it, any way you look at it, it was both frightening and thrilling.

My cousin, Virginia Ruth, quit school when she was 17 and went to Beckley and got a job in a restaurant. She was the oldest of Aunt Laurie's kids, and times were tough. Uncle Blain lost his job, and they moved over to Madams Creek. There they could have a garden and raise their own food. They had a cow and some pigs and chickens, so they

One of the many hairpin turns on the mountainous roads of rural West Virginia.

were better off than people in town. Virginia Ruth got tired of working so hard at home and just took off. Of course, I think she might have jumped out of the frying pan into the fire because she had to work harder than when she was at home. But she seemed satisfied. She liked her job and got to be the manager and made better money. She lived in a rooming house with a lot of other girls and basically did as she pleased when she wasn't working. We all envied her and thought she was real cool. When we went to Beckley, we always ate at the restaurant where she worked.

One year we all went to the big football game between Hinton and Beckley. Actually, we went there every other year when the game was played at Beckley. This was in the winter of 1940, and I was 13 going on 14. Virginia Ruth was 17, and Andrew was a little older than I was, maybe 14 or

Virginia Ruth

15. After the game was over, we all went to the restaurant where Virginia Ruth worked and hung out for awhile. Andrew and his buddies left before we did. There were four guys in the car, the driver and owner was a fellow named Johnny. I don't remember who the other two were. It had started to snow, so they figured they had better start for home. We had come on the bus, but it hadn't arrived yet to pick us up. We were just waiting around.

I guess it might have been about one-half hour till the bus came, and all the kids piled in. By now it was snowing really hard, coming down in big fluffy flakes and piling up fast on the roads. The driver closed the door after the last kid got on, and the bus slowly started down the highway.

We were all covered with snow and tracked a lot of it in on our shoes when we got on the bus. There was a lot of laughing and yelling till everyone stomped their feet and shook the snow off their coats and hats. It was pretty noisy as the kids were geared up after the game. We were shouting and singing and generally just cutting up like kids do on a sports outing.

We got out of town and started down Highway No. 3 toward Hinton. The bus was moving along slowly, but being a bunch of kids and totally oblivious to the circumstances, we didn't really notice or care. All of a sudden, the bus gave a lurch and started sliding almost sideways. That did it! A half dozen girls started squealing, and the rest got awfully quiet. The driv-

Old Man of the Mountain natural carving in West Virginia.

er got the bus under control, and from then on till we got to the high school in Hinton, we were a pretty somber bunch of kids.

As soon as the bus came to a full stop and the door opened, it was a mad scramble to see who got out first. Everyone raced over to Fred Maddy's, the local school hang-out. It was packed, and most of the kids from across the river were lining up to use the telephone to get permission to spend the night with friends or relatives who lived in town. By now the snow was several inches deep and showed no signs of letting up soon. Doris, Mary Grace, Betty Jane and I were standing in line with Carol Lee waiting for her turn on the telephone. She lived over at Madams Creek and was going to stay all night with Mary Grace. But she had to let her mother know.

I started looking around and suddenly realized Andrew and his buddies weren't anywhere to be seen. I asked several people if they had seen them, and no one had. I walked over to my cousins, Bud and Lee, and asked them if they had seen Andrew since the game. They said "no," and no one else had seen them either. This made us all a little scared, and we were afraid something had happened to them.

Bud called the restaurant over in Beckley where Virginia Ruth worked, but she said she hadn't seen them since they left. They decided to go look for them. It was still snowing steadily when Bud and Lee left to go down to their house to put chains on the truck. They got some ropes, flashlights and blankets. They came back up to Fred's, got a couple more fellows and they all started down Temple Street toward the bridge.

Lee told us later that the road was really slippery and they practically crawled out of Hinton. They took turns getting out of the truck and walking along the edge of the road along the side where there was a deep ravine. This was a slow and tedious process, but Lee was convinced that their car must have gone over the edge of one of the curves. They shuddered to think what they might find.

About half way to Beckley, Bud hollered, "I see 'em!"

Lee pulled the truck as far as he could off the road against the side of the mountain, and they all jumped out and ran over to the edge of the road. Sure enough, way down in the bottom of the ravine, four boys were standing on top of the car. They were waving their arms wildly and screaming at the top of their lungs. Miraculously, no one had been hurt. The car had slid and shot off the road and landed right side up. They had managed to get the doors open and crawl out. The car was almost completely covered

Another view of West Virginia's mountains.

with snow, and with the temperature going down, there was a good possibility they might have been in serious trouble before morning.

After a good bit of yelling back and forth, they had to figure how to get them up. It was a long way down, and they weren't sure the ropes would reach. They would have to move the truck over to the other side of the road, so they would be near the edge. This constituted a bit of a problem because they would be on the wrong side of the road and a hazard to oncoming traffic. Since they didn't have much choice, it was decided that one of them would go up the road a good piece and wave their flashlight and warn oncoming traffic to the opposite side. They could just hope and pray that there wouldn't be cars coming both ways. Due to the weather conditions, this was highly unlikely, as they hadn't seen but three cars since they left Hinton.

Lee got in the truck and carefully moved it over to the side of the road near the edge. He tied one end of the rope to the truck's back axle. Then they lowered the rope over the side of the steep cliff. It wasn't long enough to reach all the way to the bottom, so the guys could catch hold of it. They pulled the rope back up and figured the only thing they could do was cut the blankets in strips with a pocketknife, tie them together and hope they held. This took several minutes, but they didn't know what else to do. Lee hollered down to Andrew to tie the blanket around Johnny's waist, and they would pull him up. This was easier said than done as the fellows were just about frozen stiff, and tying was almost impossible, especially something as bulky as the blanket strips. Lee pulled the rope and blanket back up, tied the blanket end to the truck axle and lowered the other end of the rope down. This went better, and they finally got the rope tied around Johnny's waist and started pulling him up. This worked pretty well, and they finally got them all up, one by one. With only blanket strips to keep them warm, they had to huddle close together in the back of the truck, and Lee carefully got the truck turned around and headed back to Hinton.

It seemed to take forever, but they finally pulled in town and took all the boys down to their house and thawed them out by the cookstove in the kitchen. Bud went back up to Fred's, so he could let everyone know what had happened. Somebody with a car took the boys to their respective homes, so they wouldn't have to ride in the back of the truck. That was a very exciting climax to what had been a wonderful day: football victory over Beckley, big snowstorm and a daring rescue.

CHAPTER *8*

Byrd Was a Bird

Every summer I went to Crab Orchard to visit my Aunt Effie and Aunt Emmy. Both of my uncles were named John — Uncle John Rice and Uncle John Buckland, and they both worked in the mines. They had a lot of kids, and it was always fun there. Everybody worked really hard because there was always so much to do. Lots of washing and ironing and cooking and cleaning.

Aunt Effie was the cleanest woman on the face of the earth. She was always scrubbing something. They had gardens, too, so there was always something to plant, weed, hoe, pick and of course, eat. There was a lot of canning, pickling, drying and salting to preserve food for the winter. The kids had to help, but there was always time to play and have fun. Things were pretty rough when the kids were little, but as they got older, some of them got jobs and married early.

I think I might have been about 10 years old, and everybody was busy doing some kind of work. It was about 10 in the morning, and since I was company, I didn't have to do any work. I don't think I could have done anything to suit Aunt Effie, anyway, since she was so particular. She gave me $1 and told me to go down to the Carolina Super Market and buy one-half pound of baloney for Uncle John's lunch kettle and to hurry back and bring her the change.

She said, "Tell Bobby Byrd I want a half pound of baloney, and I don't want no ends."

I took off and ran across the road, over the hill and down the main highway to the market.

I ran back to the meat counter all out of breath and blurted out, "Bobby, My Aunt Effie wants a half pound of baloney, and she don't want no ends."

I could barely see over the high, slanted-glass meat counter. But Bobby just grinned and said very seriously, "Well, now, I guess I'd better make sure she don't get no ends, or she'll be down here after me."

He sliced the meat and handed it to me. I pushed the $1 over the counter, snatched up the change and ran all the way back to the house.

That was my first encounter with The Honorable Robert Byrd, who was a hard-working, good Christian young man with high aspirations in the political field. He was a dapper young fellow who played a mean fiddle and declared on more than one occasion that he was going to fiddle his way into Congress. By golly, he did just that.

I heard my cousin and my sister remark about how he could make the fiddle talk and often played at community festivities. He was a real gregarious and friendly guy and well liked by his neighbors, friends and teachers. I lost interest in Bobby Byrd almost as quickly as I had gotten to know him. But I do remember

U.S. Sen. Robert Byrd, D-W.Va.

when he came back to West Virginia from college, he made himself very visible in the public eye and made it quite clear that he had high ambitions and was on the scene to stay. He not only made it to Congress, he stayed and became one of the most powerful members of the Senate.

I am proud of this man from a little mining town in West Virginia. He dreamed the American Dream and made it a reality. He did exactly what he said he would do. He told the other guys (gentlemen, I think he called them) they could take care of the other 47 states, and he would take care of West Virginia. And he did just that. I think he did more for the state of West Virginia than anyone has done for any state, past or present. He kept his promise, which in itself is a rarity for a politician and is more than I can say for most any other Senator.

CHAPTER 9

Wash Day at Aunt Effie's

I wouldn't want to go back to the "good old days," but wash day at Aunt Effie's was an adventure in itself. Remember she had 10 kids, and Uncle John was a miner. On Sunday evenings after church services, everyone in the village sat around outside and talked and laughed and sang. Most of the women sat on the porches in swings and chairs. The men sat on the steps smoking or chewing tobacco. Some played guitars or fiddles or mouth organs. The kids played games and caught lightning bugs, and the young folks got together in the shadows and did whatever young folks do in the shadows.

No one went far because they all knew what was coming, and everybody had to be accounted for. No one worked on Sunday, but as soon as the clocks started chiming midnight, the action began. We kids had our orders and grabbed buckets, which were sitting nearby, and raced to the pumps and lined up to get water. The men and boys started fires in the backyard, and the girls and women started sorting the clothes to be washed. Water had to be heated in big kettles over outdoor fires or on the coal stove in the kitchen or in the summerhouse.

Everything had to be scrubbed on a washboard usually outside with homemade soap and rinsed twice. This took a lot of big zinc tubs and a lot of water. It took some serious scrubbing, too, as the clothes were pretty dirty. There were a lot of bib overalls and cotton dresses, and no one changed clothes every day. The white stuff such as sheets, towels and underwear got boiled in big copper boilers on coal stoves in the summerhouse to bleach and sterilize them.

The girls had to go into the summerhouse and wash their personal items such as underpants, bras and white flannel cloths, which were used for monthly periods. Remember that we're talking about the '30s in West Virginia. There was no such things, to my knowledge, as sanitary napkins or tampons. When a girl reached the age of 12, her mother (usually) presented her with a neat stack of folded flannel cloths and instructed her in their use. Most girls by that time were way ahead of their mothers, but it was a tradition. Not many details were given, just that we were going to start to bleed because we were becoming women and had to wear protection.

There was a big bucket filled with cold water with a lid on it back behind the door in the summerhouse. Each girl was responsible to make sure her pads were placed in there till Monday. Sometimes it got pretty full if more than one girl had her period at the same time, but it had to do. So we'd wring them out of the cold water, scrub them in hot soapy water, rinse and boil them. They were then hung up on lines, which were crisscrossed back and forth in the summerhouse. It was really full, but girls were not allowed to hang any of their underpants or rags (as we called them) outside so the men and boys could ogle them. The curtains were drawn together over the windows, and the boys would get a big kick out of trying and sometimes succeeding in peeping in the window. This was a great mystery to them, and I guess a form of pornography, considering the circumstances and the times. After all, these young folks didn't have access to the kinds of exposure our kids have today such as television, porno magazines and explicit teaching in sex education classes in schools and books. Consequently they were naturally titillated by whatever was at hand. I think not knowing for sure about certain things allowed their imaginations to run wild. I know mine did, and I was surprised and sometimes appalled at the facts as I eventually learned them.

It was a mad race among the women to see who could be the first to hang out a line of clothes. Sometimes there were some snide remarks when someone was really way ahead and was accused of washing stuff the night before. But no one ever presented concrete evidence that this was the case. Mostly it was just a busy, hot job and was a weekly ritual that had to be endured.

Personally, I loved it. It was like a big community party. Of course when I was just a little girl, I didn't have to do much work. Every family had a big pot of something cooking in the backyard, and we kids would just take our pie pans and spoons and make the rounds and eat wherever and whatever we wanted. No one cared. Some had vegetable soup, some bean soup and some chicken soup. There were big lard cans filled with biscuits and cornbread. Crocks of apple butter and pickles — just lots of good eating. As I got older and the economy picked up, women got wringer washers and electricity, so it wasn't the same but still quite a job. I can still see all those rows and rows of bib overalls, cotton dresses, white sheets, pillowcases and towels flapping in the summer breeze. Every yard by every house, row upon row all through this mining community was identical. The only difference was the size of the family. Nearly everyone had at least six or eight kids, some a lot more.

When evening came, the big job was taking down the clean clothes and sprinkling them, so they could be ironed the next day. Just about everything got ironed. There was no such thing as synthetic fabrics. Nothing was "wash and wear," and nobody would be caught dead in clothes that weren't ironed slick as a ribbon. They even ironed the sheets and pillowcases. Most of the next day (Tuesday) was spent with any and all eligible girls and women standing and ironing till everything was finished and put away. I didn't think it was quite so much fun as I got older and was put at the ironing board for a couple of hours.

I think the biggest nightmare for moms was the inevitable rainy Monday and even worse a whole week of rain. Man, what a mess. The wash had to be done. It was just a much bigger chore. Setting up the equipment on the back porch and in the hot, sweltering summerhouse was a back-breaking, nerve-wracking and at best, poor arrangement. They just made the best of it. More and more lines were strung up in the summerhouse and indoors throughout the kitchen and dining room.

Eventually, as the economy improved, modern conveniences such as wringer washers, electricity, indoor plumbing, gas and electric stoves, radios and automobiles made life a little easier and definitely more pleasant. Like I said, I wouldn't want to go back to the "good old days," but they sure conjure up a heap of pleasant memories.

CHAPTER *10*

Betty Jo's Store-Bought Dress

Aunt Effie had 10 kids in a 15-year span: Cecil, who died in infancy; Beulah; then twin girls, Ratha and Raphael; a son, Thedford; twins, Charles and Elizabeth; a son, Earthy; and twins, Betty Jo and Billy Boyd, the youngest. Ratha was always called "Little Baby" because she was so much smaller than her twin sister. Aunt Effie made all their clothes, and of course mended and handed them down till there was nothing left of them.

Poor little Betty Jo was the youngest girl and had never had anything new bought just for her. She had always had to wear hand-me-downs from her older sisters.

I think Betty Jo was about 5 or 6 years old, and I was visiting there that summer. Little Baby had gone to Beckley and bought Betty Jo a really pretty, little green voile dress with pink flowers on it and a lacy collar.

I think she paid $1.19 for it at G.C. Murphy's Five and Ten Cent Store. That was in the days when you could actually buy something for five or 10 cents. Betty Jo was ecstatic as this was the first store-bought dress that she had ever had.

She ran in the bedroom and put the dress on and came tripping out to the living room, proud as a peacock. It fit perfectly. She danced around the room turning every which way to show off the dress from all angles. Aunt Effie caught her by an arm as she was prancing by, and with tight lips and a stern voice announced, "Y'ain't gonna git no wear outta that thang. Hits too little already. Hit's goin back to the store soon's somebody goes. Now go take it off, and put it back in the poke."

Poor little Betty Jo let out a wail that could have been heard clear across the county line.

"No," she screamed. "No, Mommy, no. You can't take my dress back. It's mine. Lil' Baby bought it for me."

"Now hesh up, for I give you a good whoopin'," Aunt Effie said in her I-mean-business tone of voice. "Go take that thang off, and put it back in the poke like I tol' ya 'for ya git it all messed up."

Betty Jo went back to the bedroom, crying all the way. She was devastated. She wanted that dress so badly, that the thought of having to give it up was just too much for her. She carried that bag around in her arms all evening and cried herself to sleep clutching it close to her chest.

The next morning Betty Jo was still sniffling and holding the bag in her arms. She went out on the front porch and sat down in the swing. A neighbor, Mrs. Blekley, came running across the road in a dither yelling, "Whur's Effie?"

"She's in the house," said Betty Jo. "I'll go git 'er."

She got up and went to the front door and yelled, "Mommy, Mrs. Blekley wants ya."

Aunt Effie came to the door, and Mrs. Blekley blurt-

Betty Jo in her dress from G.C. Murphy's Five and Ten Cent Store with her twin brother, Billy Boyd.

ed out excitedly, "You'll never guess what happened last night. G.C. Murphy's Store burnt to the ground over in Beckley!"

They went on blabbering about the fire and what an awful shame it was.

I'm telling you, Betty Jo was the happiest little girl in Crab Orchard. They couldn't take her dress away.

To almost everyone it was a tragic thing, but to her it was a wonderful miracle. She wore that dress almost every chance she got and wore it till it got tight and ripped almost to ribbons — and still wanted to wear it. She kept what was left of it for many years, but somewhere through the years it just got to be a pile of rags and was thrown away. Someone took a picture of her in that little dress, and she said she

Betty Jo today

wouldn't take a farm in Georgia for that picture. She kept that little black-and-white snapshot and had it enlarged and colored. It has a place of honor in her album. Betty Jo is still as cute as a button.

CHAPTER *11*

My Steamy Sex Life (I Wish)

When I was growing up, sex was a word no one used. It might as well have been eliminated from the English language.

Oh, I'm sure it was still around, because people kept having babies. In fact, most of the people I knew were quite proliferate. Big families were the norm. This, I think, was due partly to ignorance and partly to economics. I don't know what forms of birth control were available to the general public in the '30s, but I'm pretty sure none of them would have been free. People just had kids. They shot them out like bullets from a gun. They thought they were a gift from God — and they are. But common sense is a gift from God, too. It makes no sense to have all the babies it's possible to produce in a woman's short reproductive years with no means to feed and clothe them — not to mention educate them. Then again, lots of the people who were born in the '20s and '30s came from very large families, didn't have much money and turned out fine. It's a lot of hard work to take care of a big family. Lots of cooking, cleaning, washing and ironing, sewing and mending, There's an old saying "Hard work never hurt anybody." At least there's not many tombstones declaring, "Died from hard work."

There's also a lot to be said about some of the advantages of having a large family. The camaraderie is priceless. My Aunt Effie had 10 kids, and they all slept in one room. There were two double beds in the room, and the girls slept in one bed and the boys in the other. This apparently didn't hurt them a bit. They all grew up to be reasonably normal people. They had to learn to somehow get along together, to work things out among themselves. The older kids helped take care of the little ones, and everyone had to pitch in and help with the chores. I remember when the movie *Cheaper by the Dozen* came out starring Clifton Webb and Myna Loy. I related to it because of the similarities in discipline and obedience, tempered with consideration, compassion and unconditional love. I saw this in most of the big families that I knew.

My Mommy had four children, 21 months apart before she used the common sense God gave her and put an end to the marriage. This was hard for her to do because she was a Christian and didn't believe in divorce. She also loved my Daddy, but he was a hopeless alcoholic. She considered it a worse sin to live with him and continue to have children in that environment than leave him and raise the ones she had. This was a big job for a woman alone during the Depression, but she pulled it off. She was very conscious of at least trying to do the right thing. Mommy always told us that we might be poor, and we were white, but we weren't trash. She told us what trash was and also that some people who had a lot of money and did trashy things, were still trash — just trash with money. I sure found that to be very true as I grew up.

There were always a lot of men living in the house with us. My cousins, Joe, Alvin, Ziny and Toots, moved in while we were living in the house on the hill. When Aunt Emmy died, Uncle John threw the five oldest boys out, and they migrated to our house. Ziny and Toots didn't stay long, but Joe and Alvin became permanent members of our family. Willie, who was the youngest, came and went between Hinton and Crab Orchard. They were pretty big boys by the time they came to live with us. I eventually thought of them as my big brothers. Then there was Mommy's youngest brother, Uncle Russell. He lived with us for awhile till he married Violet Dove. He eventually got a job in the mines and moved to Minden and raised a big family. Of course, Uncle Arlie and Aunt Dilly lived with us for a while after we moved down to 11th Avenue. But he also got a job in the mines, and they moved to Minden. When Poppy and Orphy's house burned down in the middle of the night, they moved in with us. They had three boys, James, Junior and Emmett. They stayed about four years and then moved up in the alley beside Grandma and Grandpa Bennett. Anyway, none of these guys, to my knowledge, ever molested young kids. We were really blessed to have caring and nurturing men in our family instead of some of the wicked and evil perverts that I eventually got to know in the town.

I was a late bloomer; I didn't start to develop until I was 13. I didn't get my period till I was nearly 15. I was 5 feet 10 inches tall and weighed 110 lbs. All my girlfriends were little, short jobs and they, of course, developed quite normally. When we took gym in school, we were not allowed to engage in any strenuous activity when we were having our periods. We might damage our fragile baby organs. When the coach called our name, we either answered "here" or "pending" if we were having our period at the time. I was mortified because all the other girls had started, and I hadn't. So I faked it. I "pended" so often that the coach took me to one side and asked me if I was having a problem. I wasn't sure what she meant, but she said she was concerned because my periods were so erratic and sometimes so close together. I assured her I was fine and started to pay attention to one of the other girls and only "pended" when she did.

This worked for two years until I finally got my own "pending ticket." I was at a football game in Beckley at Thanksgiving just before my 15th birthday, and I got some God-awful cramps. We were in a restaurant where my cousin, Virginia Ruth, worked, and I started to bleed. I was horrified and didn't know just what to do. The game was over, and we were waiting for our ride to take us back to Hinton. I told Charlotte and Virginia Ruth, but they were no help. They just laughed and cracked all kind of stupid jokes. I was so mad and embarrassed that I went in the restroom and cried and stayed for a long time. My belly hurt so bad, and I was leaking pretty good, too. People kept hammering on the door, so I finally had to go out. I stuffed a big wad of toilet paper in my underpants and went back into the restaurant. I was sure everyone was staring at me and knew what was going on. When the bus came, I crept in and sat in the back, so if I left a spot on the seat, I hoped no one would notice. That was one miserable hour ride from Beckley to Hinton, and I waited till everyone got off before I dared to get up. I looked down at my seat and almost bawled with relief. No spot. I jumped off the bus and ran home as fast as I could go. Some of my friends told me later that they wondered why I was acting so weird, but since I had been faking so long, I could hardly tell anyone what had happened.

When I got in the house, I ran straight to the bathroom and took a good, hot bath. I was so glad for the little pile of flannel cloths Mommy had given me a couple of years before when I was about 12 or 13. She had also put an elastic sanitary belt in that I pinned the cloths to. I felt better, but my belly still hurt. I didn't know how I was going to keep the whole episode a secret. I didn't have to worry about that for long because when Charlotte came home, we discussed it, and she decided Mommy ought to be told. After all, what was I going to do with all the bloody rags I was going to be using for a week each month? Those were the days before Kotex or tampons, at least in our world. Mommy told me to wash the cloths out in cold water and then put them in a bucket that she kept in the bathroom for that purpose. I didn't want to touch the icky things, but I managed to hold them by one corner and squish them around a few times till they were not quite so gross and pushed them down in the bucket of cold water with a bar of soap. Thankfully, we had off school the next three days since it was Thanksgiving and a weekend. By Monday morning I was feeling pretty chipper and quite normal. I don't think anyone noticed anything unusual about me. I can't begin to explain my feeling of pride in gym class when I proudly and truthfully sang out loud and clear "pending" when my name was called. The only hitch there was that I had "pended" the week before, and I got a strange look from the coach. But she didn't say anything, so I guess she just thought I was indeed having a longer-than-usual "pending period" period.

When I started to develop and get "stuff" and "things," I was so embarrassed that I tried to cover up as much as possible by wearing baggy clothes and walking around all hunched over with my arms crossed in front of me. Mommy soon put a stop to that and made me stand up straight. After I got more comfortable with my new me, I got pretty cocky and started to strut my stuff. This was not a good idea. I wanted to get the attention of boys, but instead, men started making passes at me. Old men — at least they seemed old to me. Married men at that. It was disgusting and scared me silly.

One day the grandfather of one of my friends offered me a ride home from work, and, of course, I took it. It was a long walk from James Street to 11th Avenue. Well, he took the scenic route by the river and actually tried to rape me. As soon as I realized what he was trying to do, I opened the car door and ran out. I think I moved so fast that I surprised him, but he didn't try to follow me. I shook like a leaf and didn't stop running till I was home safe. I felt badly about the whole thing, but I never went to her house again because I was afraid I would run into him. This particular episode put me on the alert. Then and forever after I had my guard up around men. It's a good thing, too because there was to be more.

Another time, I was working in the summer for a couple in Avis that had just had a new baby. They had two little girls, one about 3 years old and the other one about 18 months. I was supposed to take care of the kids, keep the house clean, do laundry, cook and help her with the new little baby boy. It was a lot of work, but I did it. The only thing that worried me was the youngest of the little girls was always trying to go outside, and I had a hard time keeping an eye on her and doing my other work. I practically carried her around on my hip all day the first day. They were adorable little girls, chubby with blond ringlets all over their heads and big blue eyes. It was just like playing with live dolls, only I had other work to do and couldn't play all day. I had supper ready when their daddy came home the first evening. I put the littlest girl in her high chair and tied a diaper around her belly so she couldn't slide off. I fixed a tray for the new mother and took it into her room. She was too weak to come to the table to eat and was not picking up her strength like she should. I helped her sit up in the chair and put the tray on a table beside her. She had just finished nursing the baby, and he was sleeping soundly in his crib. I went back in the kitchen, and we finished supper. While I was cleaning up the little girls, I asked him if he could put a latch on the screen door in the kitchen, so I could lock it and make sure the kids were safe. He said he would pick up one on the way home the next day.

I took the little girls into their mother and lifted the little one up on her lap. The other one was standing by her chair, and she started reading to them. I went back in the kitchen and cleaned off the table. I put the dishes in the sink in a pan of hot soapy water and went outside and down the lane to the shed near the back alley. I filled a bucket with coal and carried it back into the kitchen and set it behind the coal stove. Then I went back out to the shed and started picking up pieces of firewood and loading them in my arms. Suddenly a hand was clamped over my mouth from behind and my head was forced backwards. A strong arm got me around the waist. I was so shocked and scared that I dropped most of the wood and tried to keep my footing. Someone was whispering in my ear some bulls—t about not wanting to hurt me. He tried to pull me backward, and I was so scared that I almost blacked out. He was trying to get me off my feet, but I stayed up, somehow. I managed to get my mouth open enough to bite down on his hand and I could feel my teeth break through the flesh. He jerked his hand away and cussed me for a fair-thee-well. I took the piece of firewood I was still holding and reached around and gave him a good wallop up side the head. He still had hold of me around the waist and was trying to get my panties down. I could see him quite clearly, and he had his "thing" out of his britches. By now, I knew exactly what he wanted. I started yelling bloody murder and this put him on the defensive. He raised his arm up to hit me, and I bit him again. I still had the big piece of firewood, and I gave him another good hard whack right across the face and his nose started to bleed. He loosened his hold slightly, but it was enough to give me the edge I needed.

I whacked him again and bolted for the door, dragging him behind. I do not know to this day what gave me the strength to ward off that pervert, but I managed to get out of that shed and down the street. I ran two blocks down to where his mother lived and told her I was too sick to stay with them. I high-tailed it home and went to bed and shook all over with relief and fear. I guess I should have told someone, but he probably would have just lied out of it. They would have blamed me for stirring up trouble. After all, he was a nice, decent, upstanding young man with a lovely wife and three little children. What would he want with a little twerp like me?

There was another time while I was staying with a crippled woman that I had a run-in with her dad. They were really nice people (I thought), and I really liked her. She was about 35 years old and a really pretty woman with dark curly hair and beautiful features. She had polio when she was little, and it left her legs paralyzed. She was confined to a wheelchair, so my job was .to fix supper, wash the dishes, help her to the bathroom and to get ready for bed. I stayed overnight and helped her to get up in the morning, go to the bathroom and get washed and dressed for the day. I cooked her breakfast, washed up the dishes and tidied her room. A neighbor lady came and checked on her in mid-morning and at lunchtime. I packed her a nice lunch, and since she was quite mobile in her wheelchair, things worked out quite well. I loved that job and especially the $5 a week that she paid me. Some evenings I went home after supper and other times, I just stayed there and did my lessons. If there was a ball game or some other after-school activity, her dad would give me a quarter and I would go for the evening. I had my own room, and it was a pretty plush setup as far as I was concerned. I learned a lot about cooking at that place. They ate a lot of stuff that I had only heard about, and I was supposed to cook it. So I did. I had never cooked turnips, but I figured if I peeled them and mashed them with milk and butter like potatoes, it ought to work. She said she had never eaten them that way, but she loved them. She bought a lot of round steak, and the first time I fried it, it was as tough as shoe leather. They didn't seem to mind, but I thought it was awful. When I went home that evening, I asked Mommy how to make it taste better. She told me how to beat flour into it with the edge of a saucer, and it would tenderize it. Then she said to fry it quickly in a very hot pan. I tried it and made brown flour gravy and mashed potatoes, and she said it was the best dinner she ever had eaten. I don't know about that, but it was a darn sight better than the tough, dried-up stuff that we had had before.

One evening while I was washing the dishes, Mr. Pervert came up behind me, reached over and slipped a dollar bill down the front of my blouse. Whoa, ho, ho! I didn't like this, but that's all he did. Then he went out of the kitchen. Hmm, I wasn't too sure what to think, but a warning bell went off in my head. I kept the dollar, though, but I had misgivings. I knew it wasn't quite right, but heck, a dollar is a dollar, and I didn't get too many of them. I should have known there would be strings attached. The very next evening again while I was standing at the sink washing dishes, he came over and put a dollar down in my blouse; only this time he cupped my breast and gave it a little squeeze. Well, I knew what the heck that was. I turned around so quickly, I scared the daylights out of him. I took both hands and pushed him clear across the kitchen, and he landed against the wall and sat down.

"Don't you ever do anything like that again," I hissed at him. "If you do, I'll tell BeeBee, and she'll wring your dirty old neck."

He never said a dang word; he just got up and left the kitchen. I finished the dishes, and went in and told BeeBee that I had to go home for awhile. I had to think. I was really pissed off at him, because I always liked that man, and it hurt me to find out that he was just another old s--t head trying to do bad things to a little girl. I walked around for about an hour and made a decision. I liked my job, and I liked BeeBee. I wanted the money. But I knew I would never feel safe or comfortable around him. I hated to quit without any notice, so I went back to the house and helped BeeBee get bathed and ready for bed. We always talked while she was getting her bath, and we both read a lot. I was so darn mad at her dad for ruining this for me. While I was brushing her hair, I lied and told her that I had been offered a job at G.C. Murphy's Five and Ten Cent Store, and I would have to quit staying with her. I told her I would be making more money, and it would be good experience for me. I promised to stay till she could find somebody to take my place. The very next day, I went down to Murphy's and applied for a job. I got hired to work there on Saturdays and during school holidays.

CHAPTER *12*

Pearl Harbor

I was upstairs with Tommy Winn doing our lessons on Dec.
8, 1941. We were babysitting his two little brothers. Harry
was about 8 years old and Bradley was about 6. They were
sitting on the floor by the couch with some schoolbooks,
and Tommy and I were sitting at a sort of library table doing
our Algebra. I hated Algebra and never did know what was
what. Tommy was trying to explain it to me but wasn't having much success. I was 14, and Tommy was 15. We had
the radio on, but we weren't paying much attention to it.
There was music, and occasionally someone would sing.

Tommy Winn

Suddenly an announcer came on and introduced the President of the United States, Franklin Delano Roosevelt. He talked awhile, but we really didn't perk up until we heard him say, "Yesterday, Dec. 7th, 1941, a date which will live in infamy, the United States of America was suddenly and deliberately attacked by naval and air forces of the Empire of Japan."

War was declared!

It didn't mean a thing to me. Nothing. War was something we read about in history books, and I didn't particularly like history. Japan, Germany, Italy, France, Russia, Great Britain, these were faraway countries where someone once in awhile talked about going for a vacation. All the wars I had ever heard about were way off somewhere. We just listened for awhile, then promptly lost interest and went back to our studies and the perplexing Algebra.

The next day at school, there was some murmuring mostly among the teachers, but we didn't pay much attention to it. It really wasn't any big deal to most of us. My world was so small and narrow, that my idea of going somewhere was a trip to visit my aunts and uncles in Minden or Crab Orchard in the summer. The annual football game at Beckley was the big event of the year. There was no noticeable change in Hinton. Everything stayed the same in our school — at least for awhile.

The first inkling I had on a conscious level that this war business was serious business was when one by one guys from our school volunteered to go into the armed forces. Of course, since I was only 14 at the time, that didn't affect me very much.

The winter of 1941 passed without much ado as far as my life and activities were concerned. I had another birthday Dec. 21, 1941,

Anna Jean, age 14

and was now 15 years old. I got a job working in G.C. Murphy's Five and Ten Cent Store as a clerk in the dishware department. Nobody asked me how old I was or if I had a Social Security card. I don't think there was such a thing in those days. At least it was not a requirement to get a job. I was tall, and so no questions were asked.

I think the minimum wage was 30 cents an hour. I worked two hours after school and all day on Saturdays and made about $5 or $6 for the 20 hours. The first thing I did when I got my first paycheck was go buy my little brother, Dickie, a bike. He was about 10 years old and had wanted a bike for a couple of years. He was the happiest little fellow in Hinton. As far as I am concerned, that was the best $6 I have ever spent in my life. Soon after he got the bike, he got a paper route and started delivering the daily paper. He made a penny apiece and had about 30 customers. This gave him spending money and

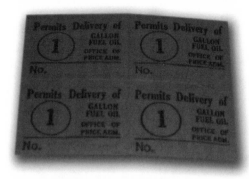

Permits were needed to get fuel during the war.

helped keep him out of trouble. One winter he got sick, and I delivered the papers for him. Everybody paid for the paper each day. That was just standard procedure.

I don't remember in exactly what order, but things started to change. People started buying war bonds. As more men went into military service, women who had never worked before got jobs. We had scrap metal drives. Everything that had any metal in it was salvaged — the tinfoil in chewing gum wrappers and cigarette packages, toothpaste tubes, tin cans and anything made of metal. It was recycled to make planes and tanks and guns and everything that was used in the armed forces. Books of ration stamps were issued to each family. Gas, meat and shoes were rationed, but that didn't mean anything to me. We couldn't afford much, so that was OK.

The movies changed, too. They were all about war and fighting. John Wayne was in lots of war movies. Movie stars went overseas to entertain the troops. The railroads got busier. Supplies for the armed forces were sent by rail. Men from every big and little town across the country boarded trains to report for duty. Almost every day, someone left to go to the armed forces. One of our teachers, Vernell Bowman, joined the Women's Army Corps. That was quite the thing the first time she came back in her uniform.

One woman in town, who had four or five little kids and an alcoholic husband, signed papers when he was drafted, so he would be forced to go to the Army. He could have been deferred because of his big family, but he didn't keep a job and drank up most of the money he earned. Now she had a monthly allotment and, for the first time, could feed and clothe the kids. Unfortunately, he was sent overseas and got killed. She got his insurance, but his parents were so mad at her that they refused to have anything to do with her or the kids.

CHAPTER *13*

Gloves in the Snow

It was Christmas Eve; the year was 1943. Snow had been falling steadily in large, fluffy flakes for more than two hours. Everything was covered with a heavy blanket of white. All the store windows on Temple Street were decorated for Christmas. People were scurrying up and down the sidewalk with their heads down going in and out of stores. Everyone had the same idea I did — frantically try to get the last minute shopping done and get home before the snow became deep and dangerous.

I was working at Krogers in the meat department, and my boss let me off two hours early and gave me an extra dollar in my pay envelope as a Christmas gift. Now I could do some shopping before the stores closed. I was just about finished and was anxious to get one last thing on my list and go home. I went into G.C. Murphy's Five and Ten Cent Store. I went straight down the aisle to the clothing department and picked up the pair of black gloves I had been admiring for a couple of weeks as the perfect gift for Bertie Spade. The clerk was a little snippy, and I didn't appreciate that one bit. So, she was tired, and it was snowing like crazy. That didn't give her the right to be rude to me. The gloves were 79 cents, and I gave her my last dollar. She practically threw the change at me. So much for the Christmas spirit.

"Merry Christmas," I chirped in what I hoped was a cheerful voice.

What I wanted to do was shake the living daylights out of her and give her a piece of my mind. But it was Christmas, and I didn't want to lower myself to her level. So, I left the store with my halo on my head and my arms loaded with two big bags of gifts. I hummed *Silent Night* off key as I hurried out toward 11th Avenue where we lived.

The snow was falling heavier now and was getting really deep. It was a struggle just to keep on my feet and wade through the stuff. I started mentally going over my purchases, counting off the people on my list and matching them up with what I hoped was a gift that was appropriate. The gloves, of course, were for Bertie Spade. Bertie was my boyfriend's mother. Carrington was in the Air Force and could not get a leave to come home for Christmas. Bertie was a widow, so I stayed with her at night while he was in the service. He was her only child, and since we had a lot of people at our house, it was a logical thing for me to keep her company while he was away. It was very convenient because they lived on Seventh Avenue, so I didn't have as far to go to school.

Carrington Spade

I wanted so badly to stop and get warm, but I kept going right past her house. My goal was to get home as soon as possible, get my gifts wrapped and go see her later and maybe stay the night. I was a little mixed up about this, because I wanted to be at my own house for Christmas morning, but I also didn't want her to be alone for Christmas. I had tried to coax her to stay at our house, but she wouldn't do it. She was planning to have Christmas dinner with us, though.

The next person I had a gift for was Mommy. I bought her a nice pair of green emerald earrings (imitation, of course). She loved earrings, and the green, I thought, would go nicely with her dark red hair. I had four boxes of stationery for each of my best friends: Mary Grace, Doris, Carol Lee and Betty Jane. I got my little sister, Bertie Lou, two pairs of anklets; she never seemed to have enough of them. Charlotte was a cinch. She had been eyeing a book *Gone With the Wind*, so I splurged and bought it for her. It cost more than a dollar, which was my top price for anyone, but sometimes one just has to make exceptions. I had bought Joe and Alvin a pair of gloves a couple of weeks earlier. I can't remember if I bought anything else or not.

By now, I was between Ninth and 10th Avenues, almost home. It was getting harder and harder to plug through the deep snow, and my packages were getting heavier. It seemed like there was nearly a foot of snow on the sidewalks, and I had to lift my feet up higher to take a step. It was dark, and there weren't many people going the way I was. Everything was so cold and still and quiet. It truly was a "silent night."

When I finally got to 11th Avenue, our steps were so covered with snow that I had to scoot the snow off each one with my foot as I went up to our house. I got on the porch and laid my packages down and took the broom and swept the snow off my boots. I opened the door, gathered up my bags and went in. Boy, I was never so glad to get home in my life. There was a big fire in the fireplace, and I could smell something baking. I was starved, so the first thing I did was take off my boots and hurry into the kitchen. Mommy had an applesauce cake in the oven and the usual pot of beans on the gas stove. They were still warm, so I got a bowl and filled it, got two pieces of cornbread, a big slice of onion, and a glass of cold buttermilk from the windowsill and went into the front room. I sat down on the floor in front of the fireplace and gobbled down my supper while I was warming up. What I wanted to do was just lay down on the floor and go to sleep, but I forced myself to get up.

I left my bowl and glass on the floor, got my bags out of the hall, took them into the dining room and dumped everything out on the big table. I looked everything over and mentally recited the people and their corresponding gift. Uh, oh!

Where were the gloves for Bertie Spade? Frantically, I lined everything up on the table, but there were no gloves. Now what, now what? I kept repeating over and over asking myself, "Now what?" I ran out through the hall and looked on the porch where I had dropped my bags while I was sweeping my boots. No gloves there; I grabbed the broom and started sweeping the steps and walk. Nothing. I started to cry.

It was still snowing hard. I didn't know what to do. I didn't have any more money, and even if I had, the stores were closed by now. I did the only thing I could think of. I yelled in to mommy that I had lost something and was going to look for it. I grabbed my coat and hat, put on my gloves and boots, took the broom and started sweeping down the steps. When I got to the bottom, I looked down the way I had come and started sweeping. I got as far as 10th Avenue, and I just gave up. For one thing, the snow was too deep and for another thing it was so dark. I couldn't see anything. I was getting colder and colder, and it was getting later and later.

I went back home and wrapped up all my gifts. It was now about 8:15. Mommy was busy in the kitchen getting last-minute things ready for Christmas dinner. Charlotte had her nose in a book, as usual. Bertie was in the bathroom putting pin curls in her hair, and Dickie was lying on the floor watching the fire burn. I was feeling pretty down, so I went upstairs to visit Virginia Winn. She was a widow like Mommy and had four kids also, three boys and one girl. The oldest boy, Tommy, was in my classes at school, and we were good friends. I went in and told Virginia and Tommy all about losing the gloves. I was still half bawling. Virginia put her arm around me and tried to console me. We discussed the possibility of another gift, but I only had one thing for each person and none to spare. We went over the list again and suddenly Virginia got a brainstorm. She noted I had four boxes of stationery, and one was for my friend, Carol Lee, who lived across the river. There was so much snow that no one was going to go far till it was cleaned up. No one else knew that I had bought gloves for Bertie, so I would just give her a box of stationery and act like I thought it was a good idea. After all, she wrote a lot of letters to Carrington, and it would be a thoughtful and useful gift. Not quite as personal, but heck, the gloves were gone, and I had to do something. Maybe I could scrape up 49 cents to buy another box of stationery for Carol Lee. It was like a heavy load had lifted. I thanked Virginia, gave her a big hug and flew down the steps two at a time. I got the package meant for Carol Lee and quickly changed the name on the gift tag. I put it in a bag and told Mommy I was going down to Bertie's.

The snow was still coming down, and it was so deep I could hardly plow through it. When I got to the bottom of the steps and realized how deep it was, I went back up to the porch and got the broom. It wasn't quite so bad as I had swept a path earlier for one block, but when I got to the end of 10th Avenue, the snow was almost up to my waist. I started to turn around and go back home, but I didn't. I pushed and poked and shoveled just enough to one side that I could take another step. I finally made it to Ninth Avenue — half way. Man, was I tired and sweating so much that I was getting wet through my coat. I had put the box of stationery on top of my head under my hat, but it kept sliding off, and I was afraid it would fall in the snow and suffer the same fate as the gloves. In desperation, I put it down the front of my dress and hoped it would stay. I rested awhile and started forging onward. I was starting to feel a little silly. Here I was all alone at night in the middle of one of the biggest snowstorms we'd ever had. I giggled and thought maybe I would just freeze to death, and someone would find me on Christmas Day. That would make the headlines. "Heroic Girl Freezes Trying to get Christmas Gift to Lonely Widow." Hee, Hee! Then I realized that I was too warm to freeze, but the image cheered me up and also spurred me on. I started pushing, poking and shoveling with renewed vigor because I didn't want to be outside much longer.

About halfway to Eighth Avenue, someone had cleared some of the sidewalk, and boy was there a big difference. I could actually walk some places without clearing my own path. This was good because Bertie lived on this side of the street, too. Eighth Avenue came and went by in record time, thanks to whomever was dumb enough to go out in this kind of a snowstorm and start clearing off the sidewalk. Look who's talking! I was doing it and had been for three blocks, so far. Maybe someone else had a good reason to want to get from Point A to Point B, the same as I did. I sure wished that Bertie lived at 790 Temple Street instead of 708.

I finally made it to her door and cleaned off enough of the walk so I could get up to the porch. Bless her heart, she was waiting and watching for me and was pretty darned sure I wasn't coming. It was getting late, close to 10:30. I swept my way up to her front door, and she practically grabbed me and dragged me inside. She told me to strip off my wet clothes and get in the tub of hot water that she was getting ready for me. She brought me a cup of hot cocoa and some gingersnaps. Well, I wasn't about to argue with this kind of pampering. I went in the bathroom eating cookies and sipping cocoa as I went. I undressed and breathed a sigh of relief when the box of stationery fell to the floor none the worse for the trip. I slid down into the most wonderful bath I'd had up to that moment. I relaxed as the wonderful, warm water permeated my poor aching limbs. I didn't realize how tired I was, but soon Bertie yelled through the door to see if I was OK. It's good she did, or I just might have gone to sleep in the tub. I climbed out of the tub and stood shivering on the bath mat. I quickly wrapped myself in a big bath towel, dried all over and slid into my flannel nightie that always hung on the back of the bathroom door. I padded out to the kitchen where Bertie was waiting for me.

She was a very nice looking woman, not pretty like movie stars are pretty, but she had good features that went together to make an attractive face. Her eyes were her best feature, wide apart and a deep blue. She had a thin, angular face with high cheekbones and thin, shapely lips. Her nose was a little too long and pointed but not enough to detract from the whole picture. Her hair was brown with slight streaks of gray at the temple. She kept it neatly pulled back in a slight soft pompadour with a bun low on her head. She was about my Mommy's age, I'd guess close to 40, give or take a year or two. She was a real sweet person, but she was a chronic worrier. She worried about the weather, about her finances, about Carrington in the service, about her health — you name it, and she'd worry about it for you. She even worried about me. It's a wonder she didn't have a conniption when it was getting so late and snowing so hard, and I didn't show up. She said she was worried that I would come and worried that I wouldn't. I think everyone is concerned about most of these things, but most people keep them in perspective. Not Bertie. If there were a paid profession called "Worry," she could have made a fortune.

She was sitting at the kitchen table with more cookies and cocoa. I sat down across from her, and she started talking while I ate cookies and drank cocoa. I don't remember much of what she said. She talked a lot about Christmas, about the snow and about Carrington. It was so late, and I was so tired and relaxed from the bath, that I nodded off. I jerked awake, and Bertie got up and told me to go to bed. She didn't have to tell me twice.

I went in the bathroom, emptied the water in the tub, peed, picked up the present I had left lying on the floor and went up the stairs and climbed in bed. It was cold as blue blazes up there, as the house was only heated downstairs by a coal stove in the living room. I soon warmed up under a mountain of quilts and blankets, and the next thing I knew, it was morning. I laid there snuggled under the covers for a while. I hated to get out of my nice warm nest and hit the icy floor with my bare feet. I didn't have any bedroom slippers, and my socks were wet from the night before. Slowly the events of the previous night came back to me, and I realized it was Christmas. I looked at the clock over on the dresser. Wow, it was nearly 9:30! I hadn't slept that late on Christmas morning in my entire life. I wanted to get up, but at the same time, I dreaded it. I was half-afraid to look outside and see how deep the snow was.

I threw the covers off and practically flew down the stairs taking them two at a time. I could feel the warmth from the living room heatrola. I wished I had some bedroom slippers, but I didn't. So I walked into the kitchen where Bertie was. She greeted me with, "Merry Christmas, sleepy head," and I returned the greeting. She had made me some pancakes and had them on a plate in the warming oven of the coal stove. She knew I drank coffee, so she brought a big cup to me and told me to start eating. I walked over to the window and looked out. Whewee! The snow was up to the windowsill. I took my coffee and went to the front door and looked down on the main street. There wasn't a sign of life. The snow was deep and untouched. Not a footstep or a car tire marred the pristine perfection. The sun was shining, and the snow glistened like a diamond field. Oh, it was pretty, all right. But it looked like it was about 4 or 5 feet deep. I knew from the night before it was way up to my waist and maybe more by now. Well, heck. I'd had enough of that last night, and I knew for certain we were not going anywhere. I was stuck here away from my home and family for Christmas. No presents, no Christmas dinner, no people around — just Bertie.

I went back in the kitchen and sat down at the table. Bertie had hung my socks on the back of a chair by the stove to dry. She handed them to me, so I put them on and started putting butter and syrup on my pancakes. Bertie was talking incessantly, but I was scarcely hearing her. I was too engrossed in my misery. I knew there was no way we were going to get out of this house till someone came and shoveled a path and cleared off the streets. I hadn't said much, and I looked at Bertie and suddenly I was ashamed of myself. If I hadn't come here last night, she would have been all alone for Christmas. I wasn't exactly glad I was here, but I was glad she wasn't alone. The pancakes were delicious, and I wolfed down four of them. I carried my plate over to the sink, but Bertie wouldn't let me help wash dishes. She told me to go get dressed, and we'd open our gifts. Bertie had hung my clothes by the stove in the kitchen, and they were good and dry. I carried them in the bathroom and dressed quickly, combed my hair and brushed my teeth. I ran upstairs to the cold bedroom and got the present I had brought to Bertie. I wanted it to be more, but I was glad that at least I had something.

When I came down to the living room, I looked at the little tree over in the corner by the cretonne-covered couch. It was decorated so pretty, but I couldn't help thinking how much she must be missing Carrington. There were only four packages under the tree, and I thought of the difference a family makes. We might get on each other's nerves at times, but by golly, we were never lonely. Even if we didn't have much money, we always seemed to have an awful lot of packages under our tree. I walked over and laid my package down with the rest. Bertie was still in the kitchen, so I went in. She was peeling potatoes, so I sat down in a chair across from her and just watched her. She said since the snow was so deep, we would have to make something for dinner here. That made sense but depressed me more. I was thinking of all the goodies Mommy would have on our table. A big roasted chicken, stuffing, mashed potatoes, gravy, peas and applesauce cake. She always made applesauce cake for Christmas.

"What else are we having?" I asked Bertie.

She looked at me sort of strange and said, "I'm not sure. I'll think of something. I really wasn't planing to cook dinner today, so I didn't buy much."

Oh, boy, that didn't sound good.

Bertie finished the potatoes and put them in the sink in a bowl of water, so they wouldn't turn black. She turned around and walked over to me. She took me by the hand and led me to the living room. She didn't say anything. I think that's the only time since I knew her that she wasn't talking a mile a minute. When we got in the living room, I sat down on the couch by the Christmas tree. Bertie went across the room and turned the radio on. She worked the dial till finally she got a station that was playing Christmas carols. There was a good bit of static, but it was better than nothing and cleared up every now and then. She got a package from under the tree and handed it to me. I laid it on the couch beside me. I went over to the tree and picked up the package I had brought for her. She sat down on the other end of the couch, and we both opened our gifts. I untied the ribbon and carefully unwrapped the box. When I took the lid off, I couldn't believe my eyes. Lying in the box, wrapped in white tissue paper, was a beautiful pair of hand-knitted white gloves. Bertie had made them just for me. It was just too ironic; it was too much. I could feel my eyes filling up with tears, but I tried not to let her see. I picked the gloves up reverently and held them up to my cheek. So soft, they were like cotton. I put them on, and they fit perfectly. I couldn't help it; I just burst into tears. I think I scared Bertie.

"What's the matter?" she asked. "Don't you like them?"

What could I say? How could I explain my bizarre behavior? I leaned over and put my arms around her and bawled on her shoulder. I'm sure she didn't expect such an emotional reaction to a pair of gloves, but she didn't know about the gloves lost in the snow. I decided not to tell her, why I'm not sure. She had opened her gift and thanked me after I calmed down. I asked her who the other three gifts were for. She said two were for her from Carrington, and one was from her to him. She wouldn't open the ones he sent her till he came home, and she wanted him to have one to open also. She said she had mailed him things a couple of weeks before, so he would have something from her for Christmas. I think Bertie was satisfied with the stationery, but it wasn't anything to get all shook up over. Now the gloves, hmm, well, that was my private Christmas story. I did tell Carrington about it later. We have remained good friends. Funny how such a small, insignificant thing can take on special meaning and live on in one's memory.

After I calmed down and assured Bertie that I loved the gloves, we went to the front door and looked out. It was calm and quiet and white. There were a few hardy folks out trying to clean off their porches and walks. I decided to join them. I ran to the kitchen and put on my coat, hat, gloves and boots. Bertie protested, but I took my trusty broom and went out. I pushed and swept till the porch and steps were reasonably cleared. I didn't tackle the sidewalk. I'd had enough of that the night before. I came back in, put my winter garb back behind the stove and went in the living room.

Bertie was upstairs, probably making the bed or something. She slept downstairs in a bedroom, which was adjacent to the living room and dining room. She had a desk at the side of the stair rail in the corner of the living room where I did my lessons at night when I stayed with her. I walked over there and got the book I had been reading. I curled up on the chair by the stove and started reading. I couldn't concentrate. My mind kept wandering: the events of the previous night, the no-presents, no-dinner, no-people Christmas, the gloves, yeah, the gloves. I wanted to go home so badly, but I wasn't anxious to tackle a repeat performance of my trip here. So I did the only thing I could do in a situation like this; I fell asleep.

When I woke up, I could smell something frying. Bertie was obviously making dinner. I must have been tuckered out from the night before and the little bit of cold air and shoveling I had just done. I guess I must have slept a couple of hours. I went in the kitchen. Bertie was setting the table. She looked over at me and smiled.

"I thought you were going to sleep all day," she said teasingly. "Are you hungry?"

I was, so I nodded.

"Sit down," she said, "It's not exactly a Christmas dinner, but we won't starve."

We had hot dogs, home-fried potatoes and corn. I have to admit it tasted mighty good. I put mustard on my hot dog, rolled it up in a biscuit, and scarfed it down like it was chicken. There's nothing I like better than good, crispy, brown, fried potatoes.

After we ate and cleaned up the dishes, I was bored again. I dressed up in my heavy clothes and went outside. It was still winter out there, but there were signs of life now.

Most of the sidewalks had been at least partially cleared, and the roads were being plowed. I debated about going home, but something held me back. I couldn't bear to think of Bertie all alone at Christmas and in this snow mess. After a few minutes, she came out all bundled up, carrying a snow shovel and the broom.

"I thought I'd give you a hand," she grinned and handed me the shovel.

She started sweeping, and I started shoveling. We cleared the porch, the steps. I looked at the sidewalk and groaned. No way was I going to shovel that thing. Well, maybe just a little bit of it. We worked for about one-half hour, then I went down in the yard and started to roll up some snow for a snowman. After I got a big enough ball, I started another one. Bertie got into it and started one of her own. She helped me lift mine up on top of the big one, and then we put hers on for the head. We had a little trouble finding rocks in the snow for the eyes, so we went in the kitchen and got some coal out of the coal bucket. Bertie got an old hat and put it on his head. We made arms out of snow and stuck the broom in his arms. He needed a nose, so we just had to use coal as we didn't have a carrot. We stood back and looked him over. He looked pretty darned good to us.

There were quite a few people out and about by now. It was close to 3. Most everyone had opened their gifts and eaten their Christmas dinner. Now it was time for the traditional neighborhood and friend visitation. We always went trotting from one house to another gathering up people as we went. We exchanged greetings, gifts and got refreshments. I was missing out on this, but so was most everyone else due to the inclement weather.

I was just putting a scarf around the neck of our snow-man when I heard someone call my name. I looked up and there came my cousins, Alvin and Joe, each carrying a big bag. Mommy had sent our Christmas dinner to us, only we would have Christmas supper instead. They said they had been shoveling snow most of the morning. I think they were glad to get away, even if it was a rough trip. They said most of the sidewalks had been cleared enough that there was a path, and it wasn't too rough. They came up on the porch but wouldn't come in the house. They said it was too much trouble to take off all their coats and boots.

Bertie went in and came out with some hot cocoa and cookies. I started to ask them to help us shovel snow, but I figured they had enough of that around home. They ate the cookies, drank the cocoa and left. Bertie took the bag of food in the house, and I followed her with my bag of presents. I took off my winter stuff and went in the living room and opened my gifts. I felt a little guilty because I had so much, and Bertie only had a few. Thank heavens, mommy sent her a package. Mommy got me a little silver wristwatch with my name engraved on the back. I don't remember what else I had but I surely did love that watch. I read my book for awhile, and Bertie started warming up our supper. I had decided to stay overnight again. I usually stayed with her anyway, so it would be dumb of me to leave her on Christmas and in all that snow. We had a delicious Christmas dinner at suppertime. I can honestly say that was both the best and the worst Christmas that I can remember. At least it is one I will never forget.

Footnotes

Carrington returned home after he was discharged from the Air Force. I moved to Virginia, and we lost touch for several years. He married Ruth Somebody from Ronceverte, W.V., and they had one daughter, Patty. He owned and operated the Western Auto, Radio

Bertie Spade with her granddaughter, Patty.

Shack and hardware store in Hinton until 1996, when he closed them and retired. He and Ruth lived with Bertie and cared for her until her death.

Carrington is 82 years old as of this writing. His wife, Ruth, died in 1998. Bertie lived to be nearly 100 years old and died at the same house in Hinton that she lived in when I was staying with her. Charlotte and I went to Hinton in the summer of 2004 and tried to find Carrington. We went to the house on Temple Street, and it was boarded up. When we checked with the neighbors, they told us he had had a stroke and was in a nursing home in Princeton.

At Christmas 2005, I received a long letter from him, informing me that he was better and now living with his daughter in Princeton. I think he likes this story about his mother. Several years ago he remarked that we should go down memory lane and try to find the gloves that were lost in the snow.

CHAPTER *14*

To Virginia with Virginia

After I graduated from high school in May 1944, Charlotte and I went to Hampton, Va. We lived with Virginia Winn and her sister, Margaret, in a great big, beautiful, white house on Queen Street, which had been made into four apartments. We had the left side of the first floor. There was a kitchen, dining room, living room, two bedrooms and two bathrooms. The house had a big porch in front. There was a big hallway with a dark mahogany stairway in the middle. It was a lovely house and must have been a grand place in its heyday. We paid her $5 a week for room and board and all the privileges of home.

The house in Hampton, Va., where Anna Jean lived.

Since there was no work for us in Hinton, Virginia coaxed Mommy to let us go along with her when she moved. Virginia was a widow with four kids, the same as Mommy. They lived upstairs, and we lived downstairs in the big green house on 11th Avenue. She was a little, thin, black-haired woman with the most energy of anyone I've ever met. She had sharp features, thin lips, dark eyes and hair and a rather prominent nose. She was a very attractive woman with style and brains. She dressed impeccably, and she had an air of authority. She was an investigator with the government in the welfare department and was transferred to Hampton. Her son, Tommy, was in the Navy and was stationed at Norfolk.

There was plenty of employment in and around Hampton. There was Langley Flying Field, Fort Monroe, Norfolk Navy Base, Fort Lee, Fort Eustes, Camp Perry,

Newport News Shipyards, just to name a few. Charlotte took the civil service test at Langley Field, but I wasn't old enough. You had to be 18, so I got a job working at the Acropole Restaurant in Hampton. I liked my job at the restaurant and made about $8 to $10 a week in tips plus I got to eat all I wanted. I was really living it up. It was a real eye opener for me: so many different kinds of food, so many different kinds of men and boys. Wow! I thought I had died and gone to heaven.

Our Unwhore House

Virginia was stricter than Mommy was, though. She wouldn't let us go out with any of the guys who were always flirting with us. We made dates with some of the service-men. They had to come to the house, and we were not allowed to go anywhere with them. We had a record player and plenty of snacks, so we could dance, eat and generally just hangout. I guess this was a little too tame for some of the guys because when we explained the game plan to them, they lost interest. We weren't wild and wooly enough for them. Most of the guys we brought home were really nice, and all of them were homesick. We got a lot of regulars, and I think they were just glad to have a decent homey place to drop in. Besides it was a cheap date. We didn't develop any serious relationships at this time. Everybody just liked everybody, and we all had a lot of fun. Most of the guys we had made dates with would continue to drop in even if we did not have a date with them. Some of them would bring a buddy along just to hang out. Also word got out at the bases about our house, and we started getting uninvited guests.

Not only was this not acceptable, but Virginia had a couple of problems. She was afraid all the male traffic in and out of our house might give out the wrong idea about what kind of entertainment we were providing. Instead of protecting our reputation and preserving our virtue, this steady stream of servicemen could cause raised eyebrows. Also it was getting quite expensive trying to provide snacks for these bottomless pits. As a last resort, she made a rule that anyone coming to our house had to be accompanied by one of the four of us. It was a little hard to get the message through to the fellows without hurting their feelings, but eventually the deluge stopped as word got passed around. Fortunately, most of the guys understood where we were coming from, and no bad mouthing went on as far as we knew. There were some rough times when some of the guys would get their orders and have to leave to go overseas. We had formed genuine attachments to most of them and truly felt grief when they had to leave. Some of the fellows who had been regulars early on came to tell us goodbye when they had to go overseas or got discharged. It was almost like we had our own private little USO.

Langley Field

After awhile I took a Red Cross course and became a nurses' aid. I volunteered to work at Langley Field Hospital from 6 a.m. to noon. I worked at the restaurant from 4 p.m. till midnight — "the graveyard shift" — a long day. But I was young and full of pep, so I didn't mind. I had always wanted to be a nurse. But this rigorous, tight schedule put a damper on my in-home dating. I was tuckered out by the time I got off at midnight. I spent most of my Sundays sleeping to catch up for lost time.

I took my nurses' aid training with a girl named Dawn Carper. She was as nutty as I was, and we had a wonderful time together. Dawn was about my height, had beautiful, reddish-brown hair, shoulder length and really curly. She had a nice figure, lovely complexion and slightly buck teeth. She wanted to get braces but didn't have the money. We worked the same schedules and went back and forth every day on the bus from Hampton to Langley Hospital. We had to get up at 4:30 every morning in order to get a bus and get to the hospital by 6 a.m. Everything went smoothly for a couple of weeks, and we gradually learned the hectic routine of military hospitals. We strutted around like a couple of peacocks as we went from ward to ward all decked out in our blue and white uniforms. I really thought I was hot stuff. I had no idea how big that place was. I just went in the same door every morning, reported to the desk, got my orders for the day, went to my assigned ward and did my job.

The Enema

One morning when I went in and read my orders for the day, I saw that the first thing I was supposed to do was give an enema to this middle-aged woman, Mrs. Perkins. She was scheduled for a pretty serious liver operation at 10 that morning. This was my first real live enema. I had done practice runs, but I had never actually stuck anything up another person's butt. In fact, I had never actually seen another person's butt. Well, I had no choice. So I got my enema kit ready, and put everything on the tray and went prancing in. I tried to sound professional and confident as I approached her bed. She looked at me suspiciously but didn't say anything. She was in her middle 60s, I'd guess. She probably wasn't a bad looking woman, but her fuzzy permed, gray hair was sticking out in all directions. She had no makeup on, and her eyes without her glasses were weak looking. She was wearing a hospital gown, which is not the most flattering garment in the world.

"Good morning," I chirped in what I hoped was a suitable tone for the occasion. "Dr. Killigan says you are to have an enema this morning."

If looks could kill, I'd have been dead on the spot.

She snarled at me and said, "You can just get the hell out of here. I've done my shittin' myself all my life, and no little stupid fart like you is going to poke anything up my ass."

Well, I backed out of that room in a hurry. I went into Dr. Killigan's office and told him, "She won't let me give her an enema," I said shakily and meekly.

"She's got to have an enema. You go back in there and you give her one," he was kind but emphatic.

Well, I got my little tray and went trotting in her room again. She gave me a nasty look and sneered, "What are you doing back in here?"

"Dr. Killigan says you have got to have an enema before ... "

She cut me off before I could finish my sentence.

"I told you before and I'm telling you again. You're not giving me no enema. Get the hell out of my room, and don't come back," she screamed at the top of her voice.

So I got the hell out of her room, and again I went to Dr. Killigan.

"She won't let me give her an enema," I whined. "She's real mad and yelling at me."

Dr. Killigan gave me a sweet smile and said raising his voice slightly with each sentence.

"Miss Bennett, you are the nurse. She is the patient. You go back in there, and you give her an enema. Do you understand?"

"Yes sir," I answered meekly and turned around and left the office.

I went and got Dawn Carper.

I explained to her, "Mrs. Perkins has to have an enema this morning, and she is giving me problems. I have been in to Dr. Killigan twice, and he ordered me to give her an enema. Will you come and help me?"

Of course, she was only too glad to oblige me.

We walked into her room; me for the third time. I was now armed and prepared for battle, with my trusty enema tray and my faithful sidekick, Dawn Carper. I was shaking like a leaf, but I tried to act calm. Mrs. Perkins gave me another one of her famous dirty looks, but she didn't say anything this time. I think she suspected the chips were down.

I told her for the third time, "Dr. Killigan says I have to give you an enema; so I'm going to give you an enema."

I turned to Dawn and said, "You hold her down, and I'll give her an enema." I turned her over on her right side and pushed her knees up to her chest. Mrs. Perkins didn't say a word; she just started to cry softly. I inserted the lubricated tip up her butt like I had been trained to do. I released the clamp on the hose and let the water slowly leave the pitcher and enter her colon. She was very calm and quiet, sniffling all the time.

After the water bag was empty, I removed the tip from her butt, and she shit all over me. It squirted all down the front of my nice, clean, lovely, blue and white uniform.

Dawn went into hysterics laughing at me.

Mrs. Perkins was very contrite as she gave me a smirky little grin. She was quite pleased with herself. She had shit on me on purpose and enjoyed her revenge.

I was so darned mad I didn't know what to do. I snatched up my tray and ran out of the room and down the hall to the bathroom.

I took off all my clothes and threw them in the wash basin. What was I going to put on? I looked around for something to wrap around myself, but there wasn't anything but toilet paper and a roller towel. I needed a shower, bad. I turned my attention to washing out my stinking clothes. After several soapings and rinsings, they didn't smell quite so bad. But they were sopping wet, and I was stark naked. All I could do was wait for someone to come in the bathroom and get me some help. I washed myself off and went into one of the stalls and sat down on the commode. It wasn't long till I heard the door opening. Dawn called out to me. She was still quite amused by the whole episode, but I failed to see the humor.

"Dawn," I yelled, "stop your darned laughing. Go in the linen closet, and see if you can find me something to put on."

"Like what?" she giggled.

"I don't care what. Just get me anything, so I can get out of here," I screamed at her. "And hurry. We have to go in and clean up that mess in Mrs. Perkins' room. I hope Dr.

Killigan is satisfied. She got her darned enema, and the results are all over me."

I could hear the door shut and Dawn laughing as she went out. I sat there on the commode waiting. I was still mad but not quite as furious as before. Soon she came back in with some of the outfits the ward boys wore. At least she had the good sense to get me a large size. I grabbed the clothes and started dressing quickly.

"Thanks, for everything," I mumbled.

"Sure. See you later," Dawn said, still trying to keep from laughing at my predicament. "I gotta get back to work."

She went out, and I soon followed. I looked both ways before I ventured down the hall. I didn't want anyone to see me in this get up.

I went to the linen closet to get clean bed linens and a fresh gown for Mrs. Perkins. Dawn was way ahead of me and already had them in her arms.

"I'll go change her and the bed," she said.

I then went to the utility room, got a bucket of hot, soapy water and a mop. I cleaned her room with disinfectant and left without a word. I headed straight for Dr. Killigan's office. He was still sitting at his desk doing some kind of paperwork. Dr. Killigan was a rather unique fellow. He couldn't have been more than 5 feet 7 inches tall and was quite rotund. The top of his head was bald with a fringe of black hair all around the sides and the back. He was very highly esteemed at the hospital and was considered one of the best doctors there. I marched over to his desk and just stood there waiting for him to look up and acknowledge me.

"What now, Miss Bennett?" he asked me kindly in a slightly exasperated tone. After all, I had been in his office at least three times in an hour.

"Dr. Killigan, I gave Mrs. Perkins her enema. I'm afraid she made quite a mess. My uniform is all wet, and I need a shower. I'd like permission to go home and get some clean clothes. I've cleaned her room and changed her bed," I was practically whining.

"Humph, I think that would be advisable. Perhaps you have learned something that is not in the textbooks. I don't think this will ever happen to you again, do you?" He leaned back in his chair and put his hands behind his head.

"There will be other difficult patients. With experience, you will learn to deal with them. What would you do differently with Mrs. Perkins?" he asked.

What I was thinking, of course, I didn't dare say out loud to him. "I'd like to strangle the bitch."

"Well, sir," I answered quietly, "I think I will stay out of the line of fire and hold the butt shut as I remove the tube."

Dr. Killigan nodded his head and sat forward in his chair.

"That seems to be the most workable solution. You will do another enema tomorrow morning. We'll see how that goes. You may go home, but be back by 10. I'll send the ward boys in to thoroughly clean her room. Next time let them do it. That will be all, Miss Bennett."

I'm happy to report that the enema the next morning was performed without a hitch. I never did get to the point where I could honestly enjoy giving enemas, but I can say with certainty that I became quite proficient and was quite proud of my accomplishment.

Washing "Possible"

Dawn and I worked together at the hospital for a couple of years. Most of the time, things were pretty routine. We went in at 6 in the morning and made our bed checks. We were supposed to take temperature, pulse and respiration (TPR) and record them. We were working on the orthopedic ward. Most of these guys weren't sick, so to speak, but they had injuries to some part of their bodies. Some had surgery for various reasons to repair something that didn't work right. Marty, a feisty little redhead, had a broken arm and dislocated shoulder. Jim, a big hulking, gentle fellow from Arkansas, who was always talking about his Addie in that comical drawl, had a fractured leg. Andy had his neck and back in a brace and wasn't supposed to move around much. Arnie, a tough guy who was always throwing his weight around, at least verbally, was in traction and basically confined to his bed. If the men were unable to do so, we shaved them and combed their hair. Then we were to sponge bathe each patient "down as far as possible" and "up as far as possible" and get them ready for breakfast. Ward boys were supposed to come in and wash "possible." There was only one hitch. The ward boys didn't get around in time to get the men's "possibles" washed up before breakfast.

One morning when we were going about our usual TPR, shave, bathe, etc., we, at least I, got in a touchy situation. We were moving right along. Dawn and I were doing what we were supposed to be doing. We were about finished, but no ward boys.

"Shoot," I told Dawn, "this is silly. The parts that need washing the most aren't getting it. We're just going to wash everything."

So I turned to the guy closest to me, who happened to be a big, husky guy from Texas. Guess what they called him? You got it. Tex. I ripped the covers off him and started lathering up his privates. I got a hold of that thing and was holding it up with one hand and rubbing and scrubbing with the other. Suddenly, to my surprise, I didn't have to hold it up anymore. The durn thing stood up all by itself. I was so engrossed in this new undertaking that I hadn't realized it, but every eye in that ward was watching this interesting turn of events. Tex was just lying there with his hands up behind his head, with this silly grin on his face. Dawn was standing beside me with her mouth open. Suddenly all these guys start laughing and yelling for me to do them next. I hate to admit it, but I was so dumb I didn't know exactly what was that funny. I did know something was not quite like it should have been. I grabbed the towel and quickly swished it over Tex's item of attraction. I pulled the covers over him, picked up my pan of water and primly walked out of the room. I didn't look to the left or right, but I could hear all the guys raucous yelling.

"Hey, Anna Jean, give me a bath."

"Wash my 'possible.'"

"Me next," and other such comments.

Well, someone reported the incident to Dr. Killigan. Before I could get to the utility room and empty my water, I was summoned to his office.

"Good morning, Miss Bennett," he greeted me cordially

"Good morning, sir," I answered him in a low voice without looking at him. I kept my head down, and I could feel my cheeks burning. I was so embarrassed; I wanted to die. I had a feeling this encounter was not going to be in my favor.

"I can't believe you took it upon yourself to disobey a direct order," his voice was low, but controlled.

"There is a very good reason for each and every thing that is done in this hospital. I'm not sure just what you had in mind when you decided to take matters into your own hands. There is a valid reason why young girls are not permitted to bathe the genitalia of the opposite sex. Do you understand?"

"Yes, sir, I mean, no sir." I stammered. "I-I guess I know it was wrong to wash him 'down there,' but I don't know for sure what all the laughing and hollering was about," I was practically whispering. All I wanted was to get out of there and get back to work.

Dr. Killigan took off his glasses. He took a handkerchief out of his pocket, blew his breath on the glasses and started to wipe them.

"Are you trying to tell me that you are so ignorant that you are unaware that the type of stimulus you performed on this young man would surely produce the results you just witnessed?" He shook his head from side to side, put his glasses back on and sat up straight in his chair.

"No, sir," I was suddenly defensive and insulted. "I don't think I'm ignorant. There are just some things I haven't learned yet. I know about girls and boys and all that stuff, but I guess there's a lot I don't know." I didn't like this conversation at all.

"I think Miss Lilly will fill you in."

He got up and called on the intercom for Miss Lilly to come to his office.

"Please have a seat, Miss Bennett; Miss Lilly will be here shortly."

Miss Lilly was the head of obstetrics. She was a short, plump woman with dark curly hair cut close to her head in a sort of cap cut. She must have been nearby as she entered the room almost immediately.

"Good morning, Miss Bennett," she glanced over at me and smiled.

"Good morning, ma'am," I muttered, not sure what was coming up next.

Dr. Killigan got right to the point.

"Miss Lilly, please take our friend here and give her a thorough and complete explanation of the male and female anatomy and their specific functions. She seems to have a vague knowledge, but there are some things she should be briefed on. I have itemized a few and perhaps you can think of some also."

He was writing on a pad as he spoke and ripped the page out and handed it to Miss Lilly. She looked at the paper he handed her then looked over at me. She raised one eyebrow and almost smiled but caught herself and said to me politely, "Please come with me." I followed her out to the hall. She had such short legs, that even though she was walking briskly by her standards, I had to almost go in slow motion to stay with her. We walked upstairs to the cafeteria and sat down at a table over against the wall.

I don't remember much of what she said to me. I just sat there hunched over with my arms crossed on my chest. She was talking about things I didn't want to hear. I knew about boys and girls and sex and stuff. What did she think I was anyhow, a baby? I was very embarrassed, but then she asked me a stupid question.

"Did it not occur to you that fondling this man's penis could have severe repercussions?"

I looked up at her and blurted out, "I wasn't fondling it. I was washing the stinkin' thing."

"I guess that makes sense. I'm quite convinced that your action was without an ulterior motive, but the male penis is quite tuned to respond to stimulation of any sort. Now, you being an attractive young girl, and Tex being a normal human male, the reaction was inevitable. Are you following me, Miss Bennett?"

"Yes, ma'am. I think so," I answered, looking up at her for the first time. "I just wanted the guys to be clean all over. I didn't know it was going to be such a big deal, or I wouldn't have done it. Now what? Am I gonna' get fired?"

Miss Lilly stood up and motioned for me to do the same. "I really don't think it is that easy to dismiss volunteers, but you must try to comply with regulations. Do you think you can do that, Miss Bennett?"

"Yes, ma'am," I responded, relieved that my sex education class and personal reprimand was coming to a close.

We left the cafeteria, and I went to find Dawn Carper. She had high-tailed it out of the orthopedic ward as soon as I did. I didn't have to look for her, because she was watching and waiting for me to come out of the cafeteria. She grabbed me just as I was turning the corner to go to the office to find out what I was supposed to do next. We were usually giggling about something, but this particular episode didn't seem to have a very funny side, at least not then. We did a lot of giggling about it much later as it got retold and retold and retold. I became the butt of many jokes in that hospital for some time. The hardest part of it was that I had to go back in that ward the very next day and every day afterward. It was quite some time before I could walk in that ward without an uproar. I never could look Tex in the eye after that, so Dawn always took care of him. I mean she did his TPR and bathed him "up as far as possible" and "down as far as possible," but his "possible" was the only one that had any notoriety while I was there. He left me a card when he got discharged. It just read "Thanks for the memories. Love, Tex."

Shaving Carly

One morning we were making our usual rounds: TPR, shave, sponge baths, etc. I was washing this husky, good-looking fellow named Carlos. We just called him Carly. He was a good-natured, happy-go-lucky airman who had his legs and back injured in a parachute jump during training. He was strapped to some kind of board and wasn't allowed out of bed. He had black wavy hair, dark eyes, beautiful white teeth and a gorgeous smile. He could really sing and kept everyone entertained with his amazing repertoire of songs. He knew just about anything anyone could request. He knew opera, modern, hillbilly, western, love, bawdy, Irish — you name it, he could sing it. My favorite was *Danny Boy*, but he always gave me *Jeannie with the Light Brown Hair.*

He had the hairiest chest I've ever seen. Thick black curly hair covered the entire upper front part of his body. Well, it was quite a problem to sponge bathe him. I didn't have sense enough to know that I wouldn't have to actually shampoo his chest every day. But I got a big lather every morning because the water was so soft. It was a job to get the soap rinsed off. My pan was full of soapy water and little curly black hairs. I made a couple of trips to the utility room each day to get a pan of clean water just to rinse his chest. This went on for almost a week, and I got a bit frustrated.

"Let me shave this mess off; then we can get you cleaned up in half the time," I said.

I had a good lather at the time and was swishing it around with my washcloth.

"I don't know," he said hesitantly. "This is my manhood. All the men in my family got hairy chests. I think I might feel naked."

"Aw, shoot, Carly," I said, "it'll grow back long before anybody at home sees you. Why it'll probably grow back before you even leave this hospital. Look at how fast your whiskers grow, and you shave them off every day."

"Well, OK," he said. "I guess it can't hurt anything."

But he still looked a little skeptical.

"Now just relax," I told him. "This won't take long. You just close your eyes and sing to me."

"OK, he answered, "What do you want to hear?"

I had my razor poised and ready to take the first swipe. "How about my favorite, *Danny Boy*," and I started pulling the razor down over his chest.

Instead of the soft croon of *Danny Boy*, he let out a shriek.

"Jeez, that pulls," he yelled. "What are you trying to do to me? Skin me or pull them out by the roots?"

I jerked my hand away and looked down at him. "I think I need more lather."

"Yeah, more lather," he sounded a little squeaky so I figured I'd better get on with it, or he'd chicken out.

I put more soap and water on and tried a little patch on the outer edge. That went better. He started to sing, but he wasn't quite up to par. I think he was still a little leery of the whole procedure.

Well, I went slowly, kept a good lather, worked from the outside in and shaved his chest as slick as a ribbon and didn't nick him once.

"What do you think?" I stood back and surveyed my handiwork.

He opened his eyes and looked down at his chest. He rolled his eyes back in his head and groaned, "Oh my gosh. I just hope my Dad don't see this."

"If you keep your shirt on, nobody will see anything," I said.

I rinsed him off good, dried him and rubbed lotion on the nice smooth hairless surface. I was quite pleased with myself.

I gathered up my panful of curly hair and soapsuds and headed out to the utility room. I wasn't sure where I should dump the mess, so I flushed it down the commode. Then I went back to the ward and finished the rest of the guys. Of course they had watched the barbershop show. There was a lot of commenting, but most of it was favorable. It didn't seem to be such a big deal.

The next morning when I went to wash Carly, "Now isn't that nice," I asked him as I skimmed the washcloth over his nice smooth chest.

"Yeah, it's not bad. It feels so strange though. I've always had hair on my chest, and I feel so naked. But like you said, it's only for a little while."

The second morning it was basically the same thing.

On the third morning, still smooth sailing (over the chest, that is).

On the fourth morning it was a different story. As soon as I entered the ward, there was a very loud silence. Something wasn't right. There were no friendly catcalls that I had gotten used to. I looked around, and all the guys were lying quite still and not doing or saying anything. I knew something was up, but what?

I rolled my cart over to the first guy on the right, and Doris went to the left. I started to say something to her, but I really didn't know what was what.

"Good morning, Larry," I cheerfully greeted the fellow in the first bed. He mumbled something that I couldn't understand. I cranked his bed up and started washing his face and neck. He wasn't very old, probably about 18 or 19. He reminded me of one of the Hartley boys in my class at school. Tall, olive skin, lean and muscular, full lips and dreamy eyes. He probably had a mop of dark hair before he got the military buzz. He averted his eyes and was acting strange.

"What's the matter, Larry?" I asked him as I continued to wash his chest and underarms. "What's wrong with everybody? They're all so quiet."

He gave me a strange look, almost as if he had been caught doing something he shouldn't have.

"It's Carly," he whispered. "Somebody's gonna get heck."

Uh, oh. Suddenly I knew who that somebody was. I turned from Larry and practically ran down to Carly's bed. He looked at me like a little puppy that's been kicked around all its life and was expecting another blow any minute. He was clutching his blanket up under his chin with both hands.

"What's wrong, Carly?" I took hold of his hands and tried to pull the cover down, but he held on.

"What is it, Carly? Tell me!"

"They're not growing back out," he croaked. "They're growing back in."

I wasn't following him at all.

"What do you mean? What's growing back in?"

"My chest hairs," he croaked, "they're getting all sore and itchy."

"Lemme see," I ordered. I snatched the cover and ripped it down over his chest.

"Holy cow!"

His chest looked awful. Everywhere there should have been a hair stubble, there was a pus pimple. Not only that, but they were itching like crazy. He had been scratching, and there was some oozing, and in some places, some bleeding. Man, was I scared. Dr. Killigan was going to kill me.

I covered Carly up and told him not to worry, I'd take care of everything. Huh! How I planned to do that I didn't have the slightest idea.

I ran over to Dawn and filled her in on the horrible turn of events.

"What are you going to do?" she demanded. "This is serious. He's probably got an infection."

"I'm going to wash his chest good and put some disinfectant on." I replied. "That ought to take care of the infection." I wasn't half as confident as I wanted her to think I was.

"That's not a good idea," Dawn said, shaking her head. "You done got yourself in a mess, but don't make it worse. You'd better report it, and let the doctor take care of it. If you don't, somebody else will sooner or later, and then you will be in big trouble. Besides, he might get worse, and then you'll be held responsible."

"Yeah, I guess," I said.

I knew she was right, but I sure wasn't relishing the idea of getting chewed out again by Dr. Killigan.

I finished washing Larry and skipped the next two guys. I got a fresh pan of water and went back to Carly's bed. I started washing his face and arms, all the time babbling like an idiot. I don't remember anything I said. I was just trying to somehow absorb the situation. I was really scared. Dawn was no help. She kept yapping at me that I had better report it and how dumb it was to have shaved his chest in the first place. Like I didn't already know that, now that is was done. Carly didn't say a word. It was all he could do to keep from scratching. He sure wasn't singing *Jeannie* anymore. I felt so sorry for him and mad at myself that I had caused him this misery on top of his injury.

I was scared, but I made the decision that the only thing I could do was go to Dr. Killigan and explain the whole thing to him. The worst thing he could do to me was throw me out of the hospital. I finished bathing Carly, including his chest. I decided not to put any medicine on him because I wasn't sure what to use. I think that was the only smart thing I had done all week.

I bathed the other guys on my side of the ward, and Dawn and I walked over to the restroom. I stood in front of the mirror and just stared at myself. Dawn came over, and we just looked at ourselves and then at each other. We weren't giggling now. I washed my hands, combed my hair and put on some lipstick.

"OK," I said quietly. "Here I go. Wish me luck."

"Oh, boy," Dawn gave me a look that said it all. "I'm just glad I'm not in your shoes, but good luck."

She crossed her fingers on both hands and held them out to me. I crossed my fingers and we crossed arms and said together, "Good luck, you dumb cluck."

This was our secret sign, and we had used it many times before.

I left the restroom and went down the stairs to Dr. Killigan's office. I stood outside the door and took a deep breath. I was scared silly. I started to turn around and run out the door, take a bus back to Hampton and never look back. But I liked it here, and I didn't want to leave on such a sour note. I forced myself to knock on his door.

"Come in."

I opened the door a little and peeped in the room, Dr. Killigan was alone, sitting at his desk, with piles of paperwork spread out in front of him. If there had been someone else in there with him, I would have bolted and run.

"Well, come on in. What can I do for you?" He looked up as I entered and walked over to his desk. I didn't have the slightest idea what I was going to say, so I blurted out the truth.

"Dr. Killigan, I shaved Carly's chest the other day, and now he's got pus pimples all over, and they are itching him terrible, and I'm afraid he might get an infection, and you're gonna throw me out of the hospital and I don't blame you and, and ... , " I was babbling like an idiot and half bawling.

"Whoa, whoa, whoa. Just slow down, and tell me from the beginning. Did I hear you correctly, that you shaved a man's chest?"

"Yes, sir," I wailed. "And the hairs didn't grow out. They grew in, and he's itching real bad."

"All right, all right, now just calm down. We'll go see this fellow, and see if you should face the firing squad or just be put on bread and water in the dungeon for a week."

I couldn't believe he was joking about this. He walked across the room and opened the door. He motioned for me to follow him, and we proceeded down to the orthopedic ward. I didn't know what to think. I just totted along behind him. No one spoke till we got to the ward. Then he turned to me and said in a very professional manner, "Now, Miss Bennett, kindly direct me to the patient who's to be observed."

I walked over to Carly's bed and stood there. Poor Carly. He didn't know what to expect. Neither did I. The whole ward was as silent as a morgue. Everyone was waiting for Dr. Killigan to lower the boom.

Dr. Killigan smiled at Carly and said kindly, "Good morning, airman. I understand you are having some discomfort. I'd like to take a look, if I may." As he said this, he lifted the sheet down to Carly's waist.

He sized the situation up pretty quickly and gave one of those noncommittal doctor, "Um, huhs."

He pulled the sheet back over Carly and wrote something down on the chart. "I think we can get you some relief pretty quickly, Carly. Just try not to scratch, OK?" He spoke kindly to Carly, then he looked over at me. I wanted to disappear and fade away, but all I could do was just stand there and wait.

"Please come with me, Miss Bennett," his tone was brusque and slightly harsh.

I shuddered to think what fate was waiting for me. I followed him down the hall and back up to his office.

He walked over to his desk and sat down. He tapped on the desk with his fingers.

"Oh, Miss Bennett," he sounded so exasperated and disgusted. "We have a situation here that, while I do not feel it is life threatening, is certainly unacceptable. I will see to it that this young man's rash is properly cared for and treated. Also the side effects, the itching and possible infection, are going to contribute to the possibility of complications. I am not even going to ask you what in heaven's name you were thinking when you shaved this man's chest. I do not honestly think that you do these stupid things with malicious intent, but the results leave much to be desired. I am going to give you some explicit instructions, and I want them adhered to without any deviation. Do you think you are capable of following my instructions to the letter?"

"Yes, sir," I said quietly, "I figured you were going to fire me. I'm really sorry, and I'll try to do like you tell me."

"No, Miss Bennett. We find it difficult to fire volunteers. We are very short-handed and we need all the help we can get. We are extremely grateful for all the volunteers, who work long and hard without monetary compensation. But it is imperative that we see to it that you are properly trained and that you follow military hospital protocol. Now you are going to be assigned to Nurse Wills for one week. You will work directly under her, and you will not make a move without her permission and approval. At the end of the week, she will evaluate you and will decide whether you are suitable material for this particular job in the hospital."

He pushed a button on his intercom and summoned Nurse Wills to his office. He didn't say anything else, so I sat down in one of the chairs. I didn't say anything else either, so for the first time in my life, I kept my mouth shut.

In a few minutes there was a knock on the door and Capt. Loretta Wills came in. She was a tall, thin woman with an almost mannish look. She wore no noticeable makeup. She had dark wavy brown hair cropped close to her head, and she wore no jewelry except a watch. She was a pleasant looking woman, large brown eyes and a full mouth with nice white teeth. My fears were somewhat alleviated because she didn't look like the ogre I was expecting. Dr. Killigan introduced us and filled her in on the situation. She shook my hand firmly and assured me that we would get along fine. She was right.

The following week was one of the most pleasant weeks I spent in the hospital. Capt. Wills was patient, kind, good-natured and efficient. She treated me with a firm but gentle dignity. She explained things to me, so I fully understood what was expected of me and then expected me to do exactly what she told me. She exemplified the true meaning of nursing.

She placed me in complete charge of Carly. That poor guy suffered so much from the awful thing I did to him. She made me check him every hour, partly to keep him company and try to keep him from scratching and partly to make sure that I stayed fully aware of the situation. Carly got a bad rash, which became infected. I had to sponge his chest and apply some kind of medicine every hour, which was supposed to fight the infection and also to lessen the itching. It got so bad that he would scratch at night and was a bloody mess in the morning. The doctor finally ordered gloves for him to wear at night, which helped some. It took a long time, about three weeks, till gradually, I guess one by one, the hairs found a way to grow out and his chest looked normal, nice and hairy. I stopped lathering his chest so that as the hair grew out, we had no problems. Bless his heart, after all I put him through, he still wasn't mad at me. But no one would ever again shave his chest if he could help it. And believe me, I never shaved another chest.

Plane Crash

I had been working at Langley Field about four months, and things were going along on a pretty even keel. I was learning the ropes and could carry my weight in most areas. Actually, I thoroughly enjoyed my job and could hardly wait to get to the hospital each morning. It was about 8:30 on a Thursday, and Dawn Carper and I had finished our regular duties for the morning. Everybody was bathed and shaved. Breakfast was over, and the beds had all been changed.

We were just getting ready to go to the lounge and take a break when the telephone rang. We waited a few seconds, but no one answered it. So I picked it up. The voice on the other end was almost hysterical and was talking so fast I could hardly understand him.

"We got trouble here," he babbled. "We got a plane down and 14 wounded. We're bringing them in right away. Get the beds ready and stand by for emergency surgery," he slammed the receiver down before I had a chance to respond.

I turned around and got on the intercom and started paging all the nurses and doctors who were supposed to be on duty.

Nobody answered. Time was passing. They would be bringing the wounded men in before long. Dawn and I just stood looking at each other.

"What are we gonna do?" she asked almost in a whisper.

"I don't know what we're gonna do," I whispered back.

I was scared, and so was she. This was a bigger deal than either one of us had ever come up against. We weren't trained to do anything except take temperature, pulse and respiration and treat for shock. We didn't know what condition these men might be in. Where the heck were the doctors and nurses?

"We'd better get some beds ready," Dawn said, "But where are we gonna put them?"

"We don't have much choice; come on."

I was practically running toward the orthopedic ward.

We went into the ward, and I yelled, "Everybody who can walk, get the heck out of bed. The rest of you guys, we'll try to get you in wheelchairs."

We explained the situation to them hurriedly. The only ones we didn't dare move were the ones with traction and backboards. We started running down the hall getting all the wheelchairs we could find and lining them up outside in the hall. We helped the ambulatory ones out of the room and helped the other ones into wheelchairs. Then we ran to the linen closet and got clean bedclothes and blankets and started changing the beds. The fellows lined up in the hall were pretty quiet. They seemed to sense the gravity of the situation and knew it was no time for smart remarks.

We had finished the beds and were standing by with our TPR kits ready. We heard the sirens as the ambulances approached the emergency exit of the hospital. Dawn raced down to direct them to the prepared ward. Soon everything was buzzing as the medics started wheeling the wounded to the ward where we had instructed them. One by one they were put in the beds, and we started getting their names and making charts for them. We took their temperature, pulse and respiration and recorded them. We had them all bundled up in blankets as we had been instructed for shock. We didn't have the slightest idea what we were going to do next.

One of the medics, who seemed to be in charge came over to us and asked, "Where are the doctors? And the nurses?"

What could I say? I didn't have a clue. All I knew for certain was that they weren't where they should have been.

"I don't know," I stated truthfully. "We've been calling and trying to find them, but nobody answers."

"This is weird," he looked around as though he expected to see one we might have missed. "Wonder where they can be? You girls ain't supposed to be here without a doctor or nurse with you. Heads are gonna roll."

He walked out the door and down the hall shaking his head as he went.

Dawn and I got in a huddle and tried to decide what to do next. We decided to check on the two men who were the most seriously injured and try to determine if there was anything we could do for them. One skinny little fellow with a bad case of acne was in considerable pain. He was banged up and had a lot of bruises and some minor cuts on his head and shoulder. The bleeding had stopped and had crusted over. He moaned loudly when I touched his left leg. I didn't see anything on it, but I was pretty sure it was broken. He couldn't move it and said it hurt badly. The only thing I could do was wash off his cuts and try to reassure him that the doctor would be in soon.

Dawn checked the other man and determined that he had some internal injuries, which caused us to get pretty scared. We knew he should be checked by a professional as soon as possible.

We didn't know what else to do because we had only been trained in the basics. We had been warned about trying to do anything besides what we had definite training for. We did go from bed to bed and talk to the guys and cleaned up some of them by wiping off their hands and faces. We were even reluctant to remove their clothing, for fear that they might have an injury, and we might somehow cause further damage.

It seemed like a long time, but I learned later it was actually about one-half hour, till the medic, who had talked to us earlier, came in the ward. He was all red in the face and seemed very angry. I thought at first that we had done something wrong, and he was going to give us heck. Instead, he motioned for us to come over to where he was by the door.

"You will be relieved in a couple of minutes," he spoke very formally and was tight lipped. Obviously something was not quite on the up and up.

"Did you find the nurses and doctors?" I asked him. I was beginning to get a little spooked by the whole situation.

"I found 'em," he answered curtly. "They'll be here pretty soon."

He had hardly gotten the words out till the door opened, and two of the staff nurses came in. They whispered to each other for a second or two then walked over to where we were standing. They were both really cute, one had dark red hair and the other one was a blond blond; I mean really blond. Both had short haircuts. I guess that was a standard military thing, as most of the nurses had short hair. They were both about the same height, shorter than either Doris or me. The redhead gave me a sweet smile and cooed in a southern drawl, "We sure wanna thank y'all for taking such good care of these here fellas. We'll take over now, and y'all just go on about your duties, OK?"

We really didn't have much choice, so I just muttered, "Yes ma'am," and we slipped out the door.

The medic, who had talked to us earlier, was standing in the hall across from the orthopedic ward. He crooked a finger motioning for us to come over to where he was. We looked around and didn't see anyone, so we figured it would be all right to talk to him.

"I think there might be some trouble comin' up over this mess," he said in a sort of strained tone. "You gals be careful who you talk to about this. Don't volunteer no information and don't talk it outside the hospital. Y'all are gonna get called on to answer some questions, so just stick to what you know for a fact. Y'all ain't done nothin' wrong, so don't worry. Just keep a tight rein on your lips, and don't try to add nothin' to the facts."

Dawn and I walked upstairs to the restroom without saying a word. When we got in we both started whispering together, "What's gonna happen? Why are we gonna have to answer questions? Where were the nurses and doctors? What's the big secret?"

I didn't know if we were in trouble or not. I tried to think of anything we might have done that we might get reprimanded for, but I couldn't. Thank God, we had just done what we had been trained to do, nothing more. We washed our hands and started up the steps to the cafeteria. We passed a couple of nurses on the way, and I whispered to Dawn, "There's plenty of nurses now. Wonder where they all were earlier?"

I got a cup of coffee, and Dawn got a Coke. We sat for a few minutes, not saying anything. We noticed there were several people sitting around when we came in, and a few more came in later. We got some strange looks — almost furtive-like, and it made me feel uncomfortable. Definitely something was going on that was not quite right. While we were sitting there, an orderly came over and informed us that we were wanted in the C.O.'s office immediately. We jumped up and hightailed it down to his office. I knocked on the door and heard a loud "Come in."

We entered the room and stood at attention before the largest desk I'd ever seen. Sitting behind it was a big husky man. I figured him to be in his late 40s or early 50s. He had a thin mustache, stiff salt-and-pepper hair in a military buzz. He didn't wear glasses, but his eyes were squinting like he couldn't see well. He had a square chin and a big Roman nose. He stood up and walked around the desk. He was quite tall and well built, rugged and sorta the John Wayne type, only not as good looking. He stuck out his hand, which surprised me because military personnel usually saluted each other and ignored the rest of the civilized world. His action belied his appearance. I didn't quite know what to make of him, but I reached out and shook his proffered hand. Dawn followed my lead and did the same. He smiled slightly, but it was a surface smile. He was very cordial, but no warmth. He made me feel very nervous.

"Good morning, ladies," he said very formally.

I was getting more nervous by the minute, as I didn't know just what was coming. He gestured to a row of wooden chairs, which had been placed along one side of the room. "Please have a seat."

Dawn and I looked at each other, then sat down.

"I have a few questions that I would like to ask you."

He reached over to the desk and picked up a notebook and pen. He looked down at the notebook for a couple of seconds and then back at us.

"As I understand it," he drawled, "you two nurses' aids were on duty here this morning. Is that correct?"

That didn't seem to be a trick questions, so I answered quietly, "Yes, sir."

"Hmm, I see. Who else was on duty at the same time?"

So far, I was OK. I knew the answer to that one.

"Capt. Morelli, Col. Peterson, Capt. Franklin and Capt. Barton, sir," I replied truthfully.

He wrote something down in his notebook and then looked back over at us.

"What time was it when you last remember seeing any or all of these officers?"

Uh oh! Now this was not a yes-or-no question, and I had a feeling that no matter what I answered, it was going to cause trouble.

Dawn and I looked at one another, and we were both thinking the same thing. I didn't have the slightest idea when I had last seen any one of those officers. We were just used to coming in, getting our orders and going about our duties. We really didn't pay much attention to who else was around. The only thing we could do was honestly say we didn't know. I think this sorta irritated him, but he decided to take another approach.

"Perhaps you can tell me if all of these officers were on duty when you came on at, umm, 6 o'clock, wasn't it?"

I tried to remember, but when I came on duty at 6 that morning, I went to the desk and picked up my chart with my instructions for the day. Capt. Franklin was at the desk and bid me good morning. Capt. Morelli was also there checking something. I didn't see Col. Peterson or Capt. Barton. I gave him this information and told him that we had gone to the ward to bathe the guys and record their vitals on their charts. After breakfast we had changed all the beds and finished putting our things away when the message had come over the intercom.

He tilted his chair and leaned back; he clasped both hands behind his head and closed his eyes. He chewed on his bottom lip and made some strange sounds as if he was thinking out loud. We just sat there like a couple of nuts and waited him out. What else could we do? We were scared silly and had no idea what to expect.

"OK, ladies," he sat forward, leaned over the desk and stared at us intently. "That will be all for now. If you think of anything you would like to add, feel free to contact me. You may go now."

We stood up and walked out the door. My knees were like rubber, and I was sweating as if it were the middle of August. Neither one of us said anything until we got to the restroom. We checked to make sure no one else was in, and then we started whispering. What was going to happen? Where had the doctors and nurses been? We washed our hands and faces and went back to the ward where we had been assigned.

Most of the crash victims had been moved to other rooms, and we quietly directed the guys from the hallway back to their room. Of course we had to change all the beds again. By the time we had everything back in the proper order, it was time for us to check out. Our shift was up at 11 a.m., so we went to the front desk to sign out.

We didn't talk much as we waited for the bus to take us back to town, but we were both worried that there might be some serious repercussions.

After all, this was a military post, and we were in the middle of a serious controversy. We hadn't done anything wrong, but we weren't sure we couldn't be held accountable if anything serious happened as a result of our trying to make the best of a regrettable situation. We decided not to tell anyone anything. This was hard for us because we both had a problem keeping our mouths shut, but we figured we'd better. I had trouble concentrating all evening at the telephone company and couldn't sleep after I went to bed.

The next morning Dawn got on the bus and sat down beside me. We started to talk about the events of the preceding day, and we were both really worried about what might happen to us. We were pretty anxious to find out how the injured airmen had made out. We were more than anxious to find out where all the nurses and doctors had disappeared to.

We went in the office, checked in, got our charts and proceeded to go down the hall to our assigned ward. The guys were unusually quiet. Normally there would be a lot of yelling, laughing, joking but everyone was somber and serious. We changed the beds, bathed and shaved the guys and left the ward. We were surprised no one mentioned the plane crash or the weird happenings of the day before. Seemed like everyone knew it was not to be discussed and was more or less a taboo subject. This made me more nervous than I already was. It just wasn't normal to simply ignore the situation and act like nothing unusual had occurred.

We walked down to the cafeteria and sat down at our favorite table over against the wall. We fully expected to be summoned by the C.O. at any moment — but nothing happened. So, we went back to work, finished our job and left the hospital with no more information than we had when we came in.

I do not know to this day exactly what did happen and where those nurses and doctors disappeared to that morning. Whatever it was, I guess the military handled it in the military way.

I think the reason I remember it so vividly for so long is because it "never happened."

CHAPTER *15*

Ma Bell

The first thing we had to do after we got to Hampton was find jobs. There were plenty of government jobs available, but you had to be 18. So I went to work as a waitress at the Acropole, a Greek restaurant, till my birthday in December. It was hard work, and it didn't pay much. Wages were small, and most of the customers were servicemen. They weren't famous for tipping. I made enough to pay Virginia $5 a week for room and board, and I got my meals for free. It was all right for a temporary situation.

I took a six-week course with the Red Cross as a nurses' aid and went up to Langley Field Hospital every morning at

7. When I turned 18, I took the civil service test and flunked it. Charlotte passed and went to work right away at Langley Field.

I heard that the Bell Telephone Co. needed operators, so I put my application in. They called me the very next day. I really loved that job. But the hours were a little erratic, and the pay wasn't anything to brag about. I started at $12 a week, and all the new girls got the graveyard shift — 4 p.m. to midnight. I really didn't mind that because I could still go up to Langley Hospital in the morning. Later on I worked a split shift — 7 to 11 a.m., then 7 to 11 p.m. I liked that better in the summer as I could go work for four hours, hang out at the beach all day and then go back to work for four hours. It put a damper on my social life, but since I didn't have much of a social life, it really wasn't such a big deal.

I was working there about six weeks when my supervisor called me aside and gave me a long spiel about since I was doing such a good job, that I was getting a raise from $12 to $18 per week. Wow! Now I wasn't supposed to say anything to any of the other girls as there might be some jealousy and hard feelings. I bought it hook, line and sinker. I strutted around feeling pretty cocky for awhile, thinking that I was superior to some of the others. It wasn't but a few days till one of the other girls just had to confide in me that she had been singled out for a raise also. Well, we started talking it around, and it just so happened that everyone got the same raise. The cost of living had just gone up across the board. Ha! Anyway, it was still a good thing. I just couldn't figure out why they felt the need to be so underhanded and sneaky about the whole thing. I now had $6 more each week, and the first thing I did was open a charge account at Nachmans Department Store. I bought a new dress or something every single week. I turned into a real clothes horse in no time at all.

I had been working at the telephone company for about three months when it was announced that volunteers were needed to go to Williamsburg to work the PBX board. Since there were so many military facilities

Anna Jean, age 18 or 19.

around the area, the small local switchboard couldn't accommodate them. I had heard of Williamsburg, but I really didn't know much about it. I had no idea what a PBX board was. I talked it over with Charlotte, and I decided to go. She had a boyfriend in the Hampton area and didn't want to leave, so I went without her.

I left Hampton on a Greyhound bus about 1 in the afternoon. I sat there and looked out the window and wondered what the heck I was getting myself into. I arrived in Williamsburg about an hour later. The bus station was on Duke of Gloucester Street, which was the main street. The telephone company was upstairs over the bus station. I picked up my brand new, ivory-colored, Samsonite suitcase and matching makeup kit and stepped down to the street. This was the cutest little town I had ever seen, but then I hadn't seen very many. All the buildings were quaint and looked like something out of a picture book. They were mostly brick and one story. I walked up the street a little piece and set my luggage down. There was a drug store on the corner and a place called Chowning's Tavern that I got to be quite familiar with later on. I looked to the right and saw some big iron fences across the street that I learned later belonged to The College of William and Mary. I found the entrance to the telephone company and crept up a narrow and dimly lit staircase to the second floor of the building.

I got to the top of the stairs and entered the lounge where there were about five or six girls sitting around the room. They were very friendly and began plying me with questions.

"Where y'all from?"

"Are you a transfer?"

"Are you gonna live at Patrick's?"

Wow! I loved all this attention and soon learned that there were at least 16 girls from Hampton, Newport News, Richmond and Norfolk. Apparently we were all going to be living together in a big house owned by someone named Patrick.

After a few minutes, a door opened, and I could hear the loud clatter of many people all talking at the same time. A very pretty woman with a big smile on her face entered and quickly closed the door. She had short brown curly hair and was about 5 feet 5 inches, so far as I can remember. She introduced herself as Miss Huggins, the chief operator, and welcomed us to Williamsburg. She gave us a briefing and showed us where to put our suitcases and personal belongings.

She instructed us to follow her and led us into the room that she had just come from. It was not a very big room, and the noise was deafening. But having come from the similar environment in Hampton, I knew what to expect. The switchboard took up one entire wall. There were 300 lights on each position, and the pattern was repeated all the way from one end to the other about 20 times. There was an operator at each position with a headset on and a long cord with metal tips in each hand. When someone picked up their phone at home, a light appeared on the switchboard. The operator put the metal tip into the hole below the light. If it was a local call, the operator simply inserted the other plug into the appropriate number, pushed a key for the designated number of rings and a connection was made. It was a multi-party system, so each number might have several patrons. For example, if the number was 112, there would be 112R2, which meant you would get two rings. If your number was 112R3 you would get three rings. If your number was 112R12 you would get one long ring and two short rings, etc. It sounds confusing, and so many rings was quite annoying. But you eventually got used to just tuning out all the rings but your own.

There were very few private lines, and they were mainly reserved for people who had a need for privacy and/or discretion. They also cost quite a bit more. I think Gov. Rockefeller had a private line, as I got in trouble once for plugging up his light. No one was supposed to answer his number except the chief operator. Since I was new and didn't know this, it would fall my lot that one of the first lights I plugged into was his. There were a lot of servicemen stationed around Williamsburg, and the phone traffic was unbelievable. The switchboard was lit up like a Christmas tree, and delays were the norm. This was the main reason girls were brought in from other towns.

A PBX Board had been set up down in town. The board was in the center, and there was a counter around it. There were telephone booths all around the room and a waiting section. The servicemen went to the counter and placed their calls. There was always a delay getting through to certain cities. They were then told to take a seat, and when their call was completed, they were called and assigned to a booth. It was a very busy place, and we had little or no time to socialize.

We worked 12 to 15 hours at a stretch, usually with one day off. We were paid time and a half for overtime, but we had very little time off to spend it. We were so dog tired that most of our time was spent sleeping and/or trying to keep our laundry caught up and our rooms reasonably clean. We had all our meals in restaurants, so that took time, but not money. The telephone company paid all of our expenses, so here we are getting richer by the minute and no chance to blow it. The first day I was there, I worked from 4 p.m. till midnight. When my shift was over, I was told to just walk straight down Duke of Gloucester Street till I came to a very large house on the corner of Carey Street. Well, I got off duty and went down the steps and started walking. It was dark and spooky, and I was scared half to death. But I didn't know what else to do, so I just kept walking. I crossed the street and went past big iron gates on either side. This was The College of William and Mary, but I didn't know that at the time.

After about two blocks, I saw a car coming down the road, and I got a little nervous. As it came closer, I saw it looked like a big black hearse. I was scared, so I quickly ducked behind some hedges at the nearest house. The hearse slowly, slowly rolled down the street past me. It went down to the gates and turned the corner. I scrambled out on to the sidewalk and started walking as fast as I could. After a couple more blocks, there it was coming down the road again. By this time I was really spooked out, and my heart was beating like a jackhammer. I ducked in a yard and hid behind some hedges again. Thank God everyone had hedges. The hearse rolled down the street very slowly and again turned the corner. Well, believe me, I took off running like I was in a marathon.

By the end of the next two blocks, I saw the darned thing coming up the street for the third time, and I really freaked out. I ran into the nearest yard and hid till it turned the corner again. I ran up to the door of the house and started hammering and screaming till I woke somebody up. A man and a woman in their nightclothes peered out through the glass door. I was bawling and blabbering so that they could hardly understand me, but they finally opened the door and let me in. I told them about the hearse, and they let me use their telephone to call the rooming house where I was supposed to be staying.

When I got someone on the phone and explained my predicament, they thought it was pretty funny. They explained to me that our rooming house was also a mortuary, and Mr. Patrick, the undertaker, had volunteered to go down to the telephone company and bring me home. The only problem was, no one had told me. I was still too scared to go out and walk the rest of the way. Mr. Patrick had given up and gone back to the house. The nice people where I

Marian Whichard

used the telephone offered to put on their bathrobes and drive me the few more blocks to the rooming house. I gratefully accepted, and that was the end of my first day in Williamsburg.

The place where we stayed was a big, white, two-story house on the corner of Carey and Duke of Gloucester Streets. The upper story on Carey Street had a broad stairway and a large wrap-around porch with big columns. There were about eight or 10 girls staying there, two to a room. Everything was really nice, and the people who owned the building were good to us. We had twin beds, separate chests of drawers, and one dresser with a big mirror on top. We got clean sheets, pillowcases and towels every week and a clean bedspread once a month.

My roommate was a sweet little blond from Pinetown, N.C. Her name was Marian Whichard. Now, if we weren't a pair; two hicks, one from West Virginia and one from North Carolina. We were the butt of lots of jokes, but we hit it off and became close friends. We still are. She had a boyfriend from her hometown, who was in the army overseas. He was about 12 years older than she was, and her parents weren't too keen on the relationship because of the age difference. They wrote to each other every day. Sometimes she wouldn't get a letter from him for several days, and then she would get three or four at one time. After a couple of weeks went by and she hadn't heard from him, naturally she got worried. She was crying a lot and was sure something had happened to him. She had an aunt who lived in Newport News, so we called her and asked her if she knew anything about James (that was his name). She hemmed and hawed awhile and finally told Marian that James had been wounded and had one leg amputated. She said he had been flown home and was in a hospital in Atlanta, Ga. Marian's mom didn't want her to know, but her aunt thought since she asked, she should know the truth. Poor Marian really fell apart. She was crazy about that guy and wanted to be with him. Well, what could we do? We put her on the first bus out of Williamsburg for Atlanta, Ga. She called us two days later and said she and James had gotten married at the hospital. How's that for a happy ending? The marriage lasted until he died 57 years later. They have two wonderful sons, Michael and James Jr.

There wasn't much to do in Williamsburg, for us at least. The College of William and Mary took up a great deal of the town, and a lot of the stores and other establishments were geared to the college crowd. We were kept pretty busy at the telephone company, and most of us were working a lot of overtime. We got paid time and a half and double time for Sundays and holidays, but had nowhere to go and no time to spend the money. We did some exploring of the little colonial town and learned some early American history despite ourselves. We made friends with some of the girls who lived in Williamsburg and also worked at the telephone company.

One girl I remember specifically. Her name was Georgia, and she drove a tour bus. Her brother was engaged to one of

Anna Jean (right) with Marian and James Swanner
on the occasion of their 50th wedding anniversary.

the girls who worked with us. She had a sister married to a sailor, and he was stationed at Norfolk. We went over there one day to visit. We pretended I was an inmate at the state asylum for the mentally ill. Georgia said they had permission to take me out for the day, and I was a little eccentric, but perfectly harmless. She said I might act a little strange, but just don't agitate me. Well, I really should have gotten an Oscar for that performance.

I worked in Williamsburg until D-Day, June 5, 1945. We were frozen on the job and not allowed to leave the building. We worked straight 12-hour shifts, with two 15 minute breaks and one one-half hour break for lunch. Then we were allowed to shower, and sleep for eight to 10 hours. We did this for three days and then we were sent back to our home offices.

I went back to Hampton and worked for the telephone company till I got married in 1948. I was transferred to the telephone company in Harrisburg and worked there in the business office till the birth of my first child in 1950.

Recipes

POTATO PEELING SOUP

- Peelings from 6 large potatoes
- 1 quart water
- Salt to taste
- 1 cup evaporated milk
- 2 tbsp. oleo or butter

Scrub 6 large potatoes, and peel them thick. Put the peelings in a 2-qt saucepan, and add water and salt.

Put through a ricer or sieve, and discard the outer skins. Save water you boiled them in. Return the potatoes to the water you cooked them in. Add milk and butter. Bring to a boil, and remove from heat.

You can cook a small onion with the potato skins and/or

add some Parmesan and Velveeta cheese, if you want. Either way its Um! Umm! Good!

Don't knock it if you've never tried it.

Did you know that 1 medium potato with the skin on provides:

45 percent of your daily value of Vitamin C,

21 percent of your daily value of potassium and

Only 9 percent daily carbohydrates?

No fat!

That's right, no fat, none, zero, zilch, nada.

And only 100 calories.

Wow! What a veggie.

Now for the good part: Assuming you don't eat the rest of the potato, just feed it to someone else at another meal. You have yourself a healthy, tasty and hearty bowl of soup.

Works for me.

SAUSAGE GRAVY

- 1/2 lb. sausage (either smoked or fresh)
- 2 tbsp. grease (If sausage isn't fat enough add oleo.)
- 1/2 cup flour
- 1 large can evaporated milk
- Approximately 2 cups water

Take sausage out of casings. Crumble it up, and fry it good and brown. I put the smoked sausage in a food chopper and grind it before I fry it.

Add oleo if necessary, and put the flour in and brown it. Add 1 cup of water and stir constantly till thick. Add evaporated milk, and continue stirring rapidly. If needed add more water till it gets to the consistency you want.

Delicious on biscuits or toast.

We ate a lot of sausage gravy when Poppy butchered. One of my favorite suppers was smoked sausage gravy, home fried potatoes and buttermilk biscuits.

JIFFY ROLLS

- 1 pkg. yeast (dry)
- 2 1/2 to 3 cups flour
- 1/2 cup warm water
- 1 tsp. salt
- 1/2 cup scalded milk
- 2 tbsp. sugar
- 3 tbsp. melted oleo
- 1 egg (beaten)

Mix together. Let rise in greased, covered bowl in warm place. Put dough on floured board. Knead slightly. Shape into balls. Put on greased pan. Let rise till double in bulk. Bake 15 min. at 400 degrees F.

My mama was a very busy woman, but she always had homemade rolls for Sunday dinner. This was her favorite recipe because it was so simple. She mixed the dough the last thing she did before we left for church. It would rise just enough. The minute she got home, she formed the dough into rolls and let them rise again while she fixed the rest of the dinner.

They only take 15 min. to bake, and of course, they are best just out of the oven. When we had a lot of people or had company, she would double the recipe.

I've used a lot of recipes, but I just stick with this one. It's simple, it's good and of course, there's the nostalgic magic that works wonders for me.

STICKY BUNS

The recipe on the preceding page also makes delicious sticky buns, but we just called them cinnamon rolls.

Just roll the dough out thin. Spread butter on it, and sprinkle with cinnamon sugar. Roll up from the wide side and cut. Put in a pan with melted butter, and bake just like the rolls.

Buttermilk Pound Cake

- 1/2 cup butter
- 3 cups flour
- 1/2 cup Crisco
- 1 tsp. soda
- 2 cups sugar
- 1/2 tsp. baking powder
- 5 eggs
- 1/2 tsp. salt
- 1 cup buttermilk
- 1 tsp. nutmeg (Optional, I don't use it.)
- 2 tsp. vanilla

Cream butter, Crisco and sugar together. Add eggs one at a time, beating after each. Add dry ingredients alternately with buttermilk. Add vanilla. Pour into 2 well-greased and floured loaf pans. Bake about 40 to 45 min. in a 325 degree oven.

Mommy didn't do much baking except for bread, which she made every day.

We always had biscuits for breakfast and corn bread for supper. The only time I ever got a piece of store-bought, light bread was once in a while at Mary Grace's house after school. We made mayonnaise sandwiches. I loved them, but I think it was the wonder of the light bread more than anything else.

Anyway, back to the buttermilk pound cake.

There was a very nice woman who lived up on the mountain, and she had a lot of chickens, cows, pigs and a garden. Every day she would bring her butter, eggs, milk, cheese, buttermilk and fresh vegetables down to town and sell them. She had a lot of regular customers, who she delivered to door to door. Anytime she had anything left over, we got it for free. She just dropped it off on her way home.

Because we had access to free butter, eggs and buttermilk, it was only natural that Mommy would make something good out of them. This cake is a moist, delicious cake that's good alone and scrumptious with berries and whipped cream. Try it, you'll like it.

Estella Hester Bennett, Anna Jean's mother and a great cook.

EASY CHICKEN AND DUMPLINGS

- 1, 3 to 4 lb. roasting chicken cut up
- 5 medium potatoes sliced
- 1 medium onion
- 1 stalk celery
- Salt and pepper to taste

Boil chicken in about 2 quarts of salted water till tender, about 1 hour. Remove chicken, and add potatoes, onion, carrots and celery to broth, and simmer for about 15 min. Add dumplings.

Dumplings
- 2 cups flour
- 1/3 cup Crisco
- 1 tsp. baking powder
- 1 tsp. baking soda
- 1 tsp. salt
- 1 cup buttermilk

Mix dry ingredients and Crisco together till well combined. Add buttermilk, and mix till moistened. Do not stir too much.

Drop small amounts of dough into boiling liquid with teaspoon. Reduce heat, and cook 10 min. uncovered and then cook another 10 min. with lid on. Keep heat low so steam won't escape, and let dumplings get soggy.

Believe it or not chicken is the one thing that I can remember costing more when I was a kid than it does now. Chicken was a luxury reserved for special occasions such as Christmas and Thanksgiving. Grandma Bennett raised some and made chicken and dumplings more often than Mommy did. It's still one of my favorite meals — if it's made right.